Complicated Kris Northern

"This image illustrates some of the best qualities of fractals—infinity, reiteration, and self similarity."– **Kris Northern**

Investigations
IN NUMBER, DATA, AND SPACE®

Editorial offices: Glenview, Illinois • Parsippany, New Jersey • New York, New York
Sales offices: Boston, Massachusetts • Duluth, Georgia
Glenview, Illinois • Coppell, Texas • Sacramento, California • Mesa, Arizona

The Investigations curriculum was developed by TERC, Cambridge, MA.

This material is based on work supported by the National Science Foundation ("NSF") under Grant No.ESI-0095450. Any opinions, findings, and conclusions or recommendations expressed in this material are those of the author(s) and do not necessarily reflect the views of the National Science Foundation.

ISBN: 0-328-24089-3

ISBN: 978-0-328-24089-0

14 15 16 17-V082-17 16 15 14 13 12

Contents

Math Words and Ideas

Number and Operations

Contents

Contents

Measurement

Games

Games Chart — 159

The *Student Math Handbook* is a reference book.
It has two sections.

Math Words and Ideas

These pages illustrate important math words and ideas that you have been learning about in math class. You can use these pages to think about or review a math topic. Important terms are identified and related problems are provided.

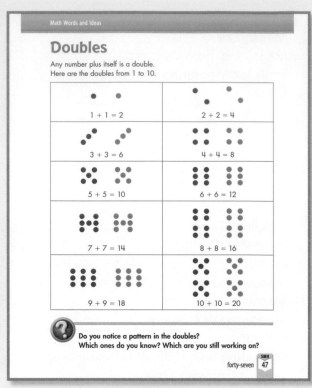

▲ Student Math Handbook, p. 47

Games

You can use the Games pages to go over game rules during class or at home. They also list the materials and recording sheets needed to play each game.

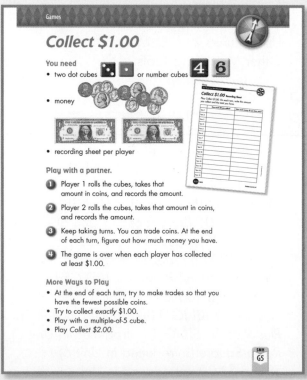

▲ Student Math Handbook, p. G5

Daily Practice and **Homework** pages list useful *Student Math Handbook* (SMH) pages.

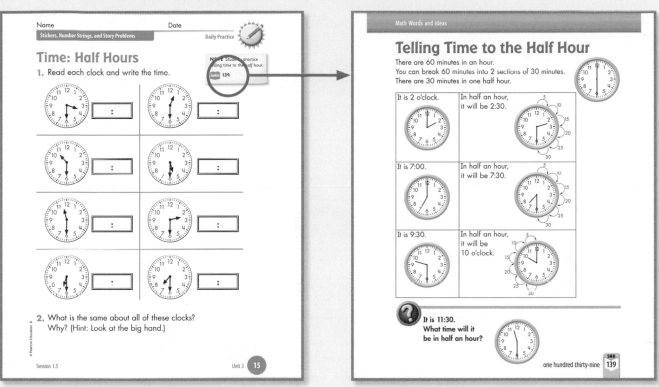

▲ Student Activity Book, p. Unit 3, p. 15

▲ Student Math Handbook, p. 139

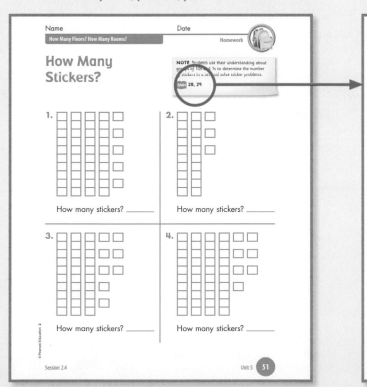

▲ Student Activity Book, Unit 5, p. 51

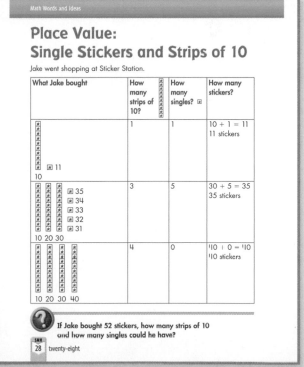

▲ Student Math Handbook, p. 28

SMH

Numbers

0	zero	
1	one	
2	two	
3	three	
4	four	
5	five	
6	six	
7	seven	
8	eight	
9	nine	

10	ten	
11	eleven	10 +
12	twelve	10 +
13	thirteen	10 +
14	fourteen	10 +
15	fifteen	10 +
16	sixteen	10 +
17	seventeen	10 +
18	eighteen	10 +
19	nineteen	10 +

20	twenty	
21	twenty-one	20 + ▪
22	twenty-two	20 + ▪▪
23	twenty-three	20 + ▪▪▪
24	twenty-four	20 + ▪▪▪▪
25	twenty-five	20 + ▪▪▪▪▪
26	twenty-six	20 + ▪▪▪▪▪▪
27	twenty-seven	20 + ▪▪▪▪▪▪▪
28	twenty-eight	20 + ▪▪▪▪▪▪▪▪
29	twenty-nine	20 + ▪▪▪▪▪▪▪▪▪

30	thirty	
31	thirty-one	30 +
32	thirty-two	30 +
33	thirty-three	30 +
34	thirty-four	30 +
35	thirty-five	30 +
36	thirty-six	30 +
37	thirty-seven	30 +
38	thirty-eight	30 +
39	thirty-nine	30 +

40	forty	
41	forty-one	40 + ▪
42	forty-two	40 + ▪▪
43	forty-three	40 + ▪▪▪
44	forty-four	40 + ▪▪▪▪
45	forty-five	40 + ▪▪▪▪▪
46	forty-six	40 + ▪▪▪▪▪▫
47	forty-seven	40 + ▪▪▪▪▪▫▫
48	forty-eight	40 + ▪▪▪▪▪▫▫▫
49	forty-nine	40 + ▪▪▪▪▪▫▫▫▫

50	fifty	
51	fifty-one	50 + ▪
52	fifty-two	50 + ▪▪
53	fifty-three	50 + ▪▪▪
54	fifty-four	50 + ▪▪▪▪
55	fifty-five	50 + ▪▪▪▪▪
56	fifty-six	50 + ▪▪▪▪▪
57	fifty-seven	50 + ▪▪▪▪▪▪▪
58	fifty-eight	50 + ▪▪▪▪▪▪▪▪
59	fifty-nine	50 + ▪▪▪▪▪▪▪▪▪

60	sixty	
61	sixty-one	60 + ▫
62	sixty-two	60 + ▫▫
63	sixty-three	60 + ▫▫▫
64	sixty-four	60 + ▫▫▫▫
65	sixty-five	60 + ▫▫▫▫▫
66	sixty-six	60 + ▫▫▫▫▫▫
67	sixty-seven	60 + ▫▫▫▫▫▫▫
68	sixty-eight	60 + ▫▫▫▫▫▫▫▫
69	sixty-nine	60 + ▫▫▫▫▫▫▫▫▫

70	seventy	
71	seventy-one	70 + ▪
72	seventy-two	70 + ▪▪
73	seventy-three	70 + ▪▪▪
74	seventy-four	70 + ▪▪▪▪
75	seventy-five	70 + ▪▪▪▪▪
76	seventy-six	70 + ▪▪▪▪▪▪
77	seventy-seven	70 + ▪▪▪▪▪▪▪
78	seventy-eight	70 + ▪▪▪▪▪▪▪▪
79	seventy-nine	70 + ▪▪▪▪▪▪▪▪▪

80	eighty	
81	eighty-one	80 +
82	eighty-two	80 +
83	eighty-three	80 +
84	eighty-four	80 +
85	eighty-five	80 +
86	eighty-six	80 +
87	eighty-seven	80 +
88	eighty-eight	80 +
89	eighty-nine	80 +

90	ninety	
91	ninety-one	90 + ▪
92	ninety-two	90 + ▪▪
93	ninety-three	90 + ▪▪▪
94	ninety-four	90 + ▪▪▪▪
95	ninety-five	90 + ▪▪▪▪▪
96	ninety-six	90 + ▪▪▪▪▪▪
97	ninety-seven	90 + ▪▪▪▪▪▪▪
98	ninety-eight	90 + ▪▪▪▪▪▪▪▪
99	ninety-nine	90 + ▪▪▪▪▪▪▪▪▪

100	one hundred	
101	one hundred one	$100 +$
102	one hundred two	$100 +$
103	one hundred three	$100 +$
104	one hundred four	$100 +$
105	one hundred five	$100 +$
106	one hundred six	$100 +$
107	one hundred seven	$100 +$
108	one hundred eight	$100 +$
109	one hundred nine	$100 +$

110	one hundred ten	
111	one hundred eleven	110 + ▢
112	one hundred twelve	110 + ▢▢
113	one hundred thirteen	110 + ▢▢▢
114	one hundred fourteen	110 + ▢▢▢▢
115	one hundred fifteen	110 + ▢▢▢▢▢
116	one hundred sixteen	110 + ▢▢▢▢▢▢
117	one hundred seventeen	110 + ▢▢▢▢▢▢▢
118	one hundred eighteen	110 + ▢▢▢▢▢▢▢▢
119	one hundred nineteen	110 + ▢▢▢▢▢▢▢▢▢

120	one hundred twenty	
121	one hundred twenty-one	120 +
122	one hundred twenty-two	120 +
123	one hundred twenty-three	120 +
124	one hundred twenty-four	120 +
125	one hundred twenty-five	120 +
126	one hundred twenty-six	120 +
127	one hundred twenty-seven	120 +
128	one hundred twenty-eight	120 +
129	one hundred twenty-nine	120 +

Coin Values

This is the money we use in the United States. Each coin has a name and value. Each coin is worth a certain number of pennies.

Money	Name	Value	How Many Pennies?
	penny	1¢ 1 cent	
	nickel	5¢ 5 cents	
	dime	10¢ 10 cents	
	quarter	25¢ 25 cents $0.25	
	dollar	100¢ 1 dollar $1.00	

Is a bigger coin always worth more?

Coin Equivalencies

A penny is 1¢.	
A nickel is 5¢.	Another way to make 5¢:
A dime is 10¢.	Another way to make 10¢:
A quarter is 25¢.	Another way to make 25¢:

What are other ways to make 25¢?
How can you make 50¢?

Ways to Make a Dollar

Here are some ways to make one dollar.

One dollar bill is worth one dollar.

Four quarters are worth one dollar.

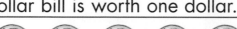

10 dimes are worth one dollar.

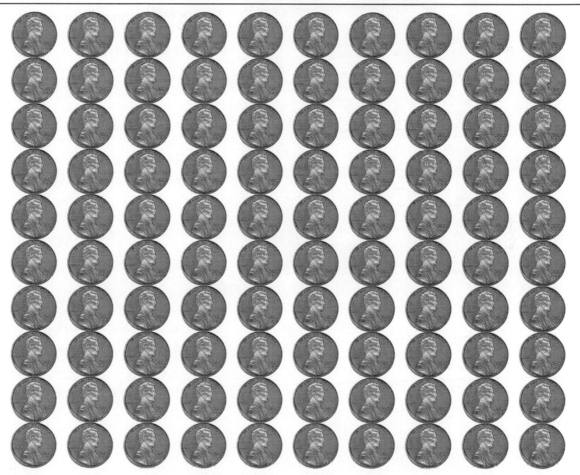

100 pennies are worth one dollar.

**How many nickels do you need to make a dollar?
What are other ways to make 1 dollar with coins?**

Calculator

Math Words
• **calculator**

A calculator is a tool that can help you add, subtract, and double-check.

The calculator screen

The SUBTRACTION key; press this key to subtract.

The ADDITION key; press this key to add.

The ON key; press this key to turn the calculator on.

The EQUAL key; press this key to see the results of your calculation.

The CLEAR key; press this key to clear the numbers from the screen.

Number Line

A number line is a tool that shows numbers in order.

It goes on forever in both directions.

It can help you write and order numbers, count, add, and subtract.

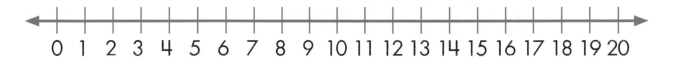

You can use the number line to count forward. You do not have to start with 1. For example, you can start at 27 and count to 35.

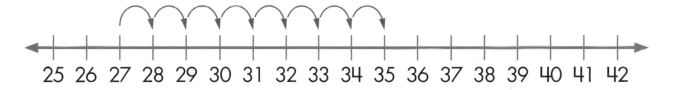

You can use the number line to count back from any number. For example, you can count back from 29 to 20.

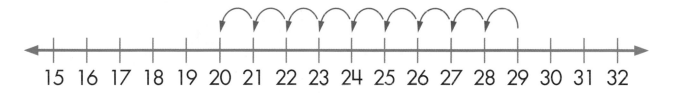

When do you use a number line?

100 Chart

The 100 chart is a tool that shows numbers from 1 to 100 in order. It can help you count, add, and subtract.

Math Words
- column
- row

column ↓

1	2	3	4	5	6	7	8	9	10
11	12	13	14	15	16	17	18	19	20
21	22	23	24	25	26	27	28	29	30
31	32	33	34	35	36	37	38	39	40
41	42	43	44	45	46	47	48	49	50
51	52	53	54	55	56	57	58	59	60
61	62	63	64	65	66	67	68	69	70
71	72	73	74	75	76	77	78	79	80
81	82	83	84	85	86	87	88	89	90
91	92	93	94	95	96	97	98	99	100

row → (points to row with 31–40)

How many rows are there?
How many numbers are in each row?
How many columns are there?
How many numbers are in each column?

Patterns on the 100 Chart

What patterns do you notice in the numbers from 1 to 100?

Except for 40 and 50, all the numbers in the 40s are in one row.

1	2	3	4	5	6	7	8	9	10
11	12	13	14	15	16	17	18	19	20
21	22	23	24	25	26	27	28	29	30
31	32	33	34	35	36	37	38	39	40
41	42	43	44	45	46	47	48	49	50
51	52	53	54	55	56	57	58	59	60
61	62	63	64	65	66	67	68	69	70
71	72	73	74	75	76	77	78	79	80
81	82	83	84	85	86	87	88	89	90
91	92	93	94	95	96	97	98	99	100

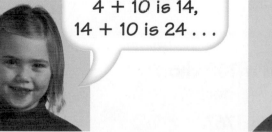

As you go down a column, you add 10. 4 + 10 is 14, 14 + 10 is 24 . . .

Those are the counting by 10 numbers.

200 Chart

Here is a 200 chart.

1	2	3	4	5	6	7	8	9	10
11	12	13	14	15	16	17	18	19	20
21	22	23	24	25	26	27	28	29	30
31	32	33	34	35	36	37	38	39	40
41	42	43	44	45	46	47	48	49	50
51	52	53	54	55	56	57	58	59	60
61	62	63	64	65	66	67	68	69	70
71	72	73	74	75	76	77	78	79	80
81	82	83	84	85	86	87	88	89	90
91	92	93	94	95	96	97	98	99	100
101	102	103	104	105	106	107	108	109	110
111	112	113	114	115	116	117	118	119	120
121	122	123	124	125	126	127	128	129	130
131	132	133	134	135	136	137	138	139	140
141	142	143	144	145	146	147	148	149	150
151	152	153	154	155	156	157	158	159	160
161	162	163	164	165	166	167	168	169	170
171	172	173	174	175	176	177	178	179	180
181	182	183	184	185	186	187	188	189	190
191	192	193	194	195	196	197	198	199	200

How is it the same as a 100 chart?
How is it different?
Where is 76? Where is 176?

Place Value: Sticker Station

Sticker Station is a place that sells stickers.

At Sticker Station, you can buy single stickers, strips of ten stickers, or sheets of one hundred stickers.

1 sheet of one hundred
100 stickers

1 strip of ten
10 stickers

1 single
1 sticker

How many singles are in one strip of 10?

How many strips of 10 are in one sheet of 100?

Place Value: Single Stickers and Strips of 10

Jake went shopping at Sticker Station.

What Jake bought	How many strips of 10?	How many singles?	How many stickers?
⭐(strip of 10) ⭐ 11 10	1	1	10 + 1 = 11 11 stickers
⭐⭐⭐ ⭐ 35 ⭐ 34 ⭐ 33 ⭐ 32 ⭐ 31 10 20 30	3	5	30 + 5 = 35 35 stickers
⭐⭐⭐⭐ 10 20 30 40	4	0	40 + 0 = 40 40 stickers

If Jake bought 52 stickers, how many strips of 10 and how many singles could he have?

Place Value: Tens and Ones

Here is the number thirty-five.

$$30 + 5 = 35$$

| The 3 is in the **tens** place. The 3 tells us there are 3 groups of 10 or 30 in 35. | **35** | The 5 is in the **ones** place. The 5 tells us there are 5 ones in 35. |

How many tens are in 45?

How many are in the ones place in 17?

Place Value: Single Stickers, Strips of 10, and Sheets of 100

Sally went shopping at Sticker Station.

What Sally bought	How many sheets?	How many strips of 10?	How many singles?	How many stickers?
10 20 30 40 50 60 62	0	6	2	60 + 2 = 62 62 stickers
100 110 112	1	1	2	100 + 10 + 2 = 112 112 stickers
100 110 120 124	1	2	4	100 + 20 + 4 = 124 124 stickers

If Sally bought 86 stickers, how many singles, strips of 10, and sheets of 100 could she have? What if she bought 123 stickers?

Place Value: Hundreds, Tens, and Ones

Math Words
• **hundreds**
• **tens**
• **ones**

Here is the number one hundred twenty-four.

$$100 + 20 + 4 = 124$$

124

The 1 is in the **hundreds** place. The 1 means there is 1 group of 100 in 124.

The 2 is in the **tens** place. The 2 means there are 2 groups of 10 in 124.

The 4 is in the **ones** place. The 4 means there are 4 ones in 124.

How many groups of 100 are in 206?
How many tens? How many ones?

Place Value: Representing Stickers

In class, we use stickers to represent 100s, 10s, and 1s.

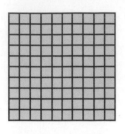

Sheet of 100   Strip of 10   1 Single

When we record, we use a quick way to show stickers.

100   10   1

Look at this representation of 132 stickers.

equation: 100   +   30   +   2   =   132

How would you show 76 stickers?
How would you show 125 stickers?

Counting (page 1 of 2)

People count every day. They count to find out how many.
When you count, you say one number for each object.
You need to keep track of what you are counting.
The last number you say is the total. The total tells you
how many are in the group.

Look at how some children count by 1s.

Jake touches each button as
he counts it.

Sally puts each button in the cup
as she counts it.

Kira arranges the buttons in a row
to count.

Franco puts them in groups of 2
to double-check.

What do you do when you count?

Counting (page 2 of 2)

Look at these pennies.

They are mixed up.

They are hard to count.

Here are some different ways to organize the pennies so that they are easier to count.

? **Which group of pennies is easiest for you to count?**

Counting by Groups (page 1 of 2)

You can count more quickly if you count by groups.
Each time you say a number, you add another group.

Every group must have the same number of objects in it.

Each hand has 5 fingers. You can count by 5s to find the total number of fingers. You say every fifth number when you count by 5s.

Counting fingers by 5s

 5  10  15 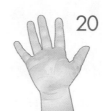 20

Counting shoes by 2s

2   4   6   8

Counting toes by 10s

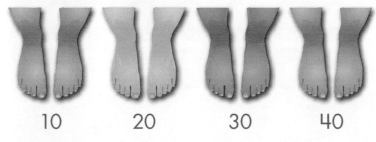

10   20   30   40

 How many eyes would 10 people have in all?

Counting by Groups (page 2 of 2)

Here are 23 pennies.

You can count the pennies in different ways.

Counting by 2s

2   4   6   8   10   12   14   16   18   20   22   23

Counting by 5s

5   10   15   20   23

Counting by 10s

10   20   23

Count out 18 pennies. Count them by 2s. Now count them by 5s. How else could you count 18 pennies?

Counting by 2s

Many things come in groups of 2. For example, shoes come in groups of 2. You can count by 2s to figure out how many shoes.

How many shoes?

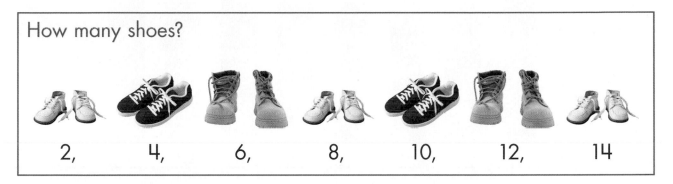

2,   4,   6,   8,   10,   12,   14

This 100 chart shows counting by groups of 2. If you say only the shaded numbers, you are counting by groups of 2.

The numbers you say are also called multiples of 2.

1	2	3	4	5	6	7	8	9	10
11	12	13	14	15	16	17	18	19	20
21	22	23	24	25	26	27	28	29	30
31	32	33	34	35	36	37	38	39	40
41	42	43	44	45	46	47	48	49	50
51	52	53	54	55	56	57	58	59	60
61	62	63	64	65	66	67	68	69	70
71	72	73	74	75	76	77	78	79	80
81	82	83	84	85	86	87	88	89	90
91	92	93	94	95	96	97	98	99	100

2, 4, 6, 8, 10, 12, 14 . . . 96, 98, 100.

A number line can also show counting by 2s.

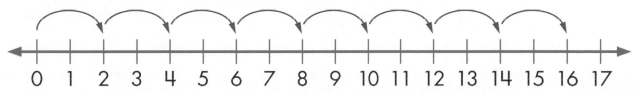

0 1 2 3 4 5 6 7 8 9 10 11 12 13 14 15 16 17

Counting by 5s

Each tower has 5 cubes. You can count the cubes by 5s.

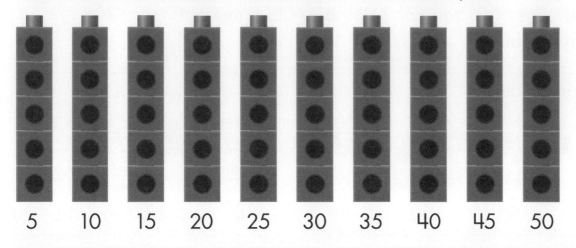

5   10   15   20   25   30   35   40   45   50

This 100 chart shows counting by groups of 5. The shaded numbers are multiples of 5.

1	2	3	4	5	6	7	8	9	10
11	12	13	14	15	16	17	18	19	20
21	22	23	24	25	26	27	28	29	30
31	32	33	34	35	36	37	38	39	40
41	42	43	44	45	46	47	48	49	50
51	52	53	54	55	56	57	58	59	60
61	62	63	64	65	66	67	68	69	70
71	72	73	74	75	76	77	78	79	80
81	82	83	84	85	86	87	88	89	90
91	92	93	94	95	96	97	98	99	100

5, 10, 15, 20 . . . 85, 90, 95, 100.

A number line can also show counting by 5s.

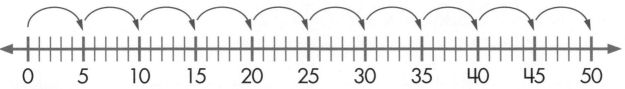

0   5   10   15   20   25   30   35   40   45   50

How many groups of 5 are in 100?

Counting by 10s

Many things come in groups of 10. For example, people have 10 fingers. You can count by groups of 10 to figure out how many fingers a group of people has.

| 10 | 20 | 30 | 40 | 50 |

How many fingers do these people have altogether?
How many fingers does your family have?

This 100 chart shows counting by groups of 10.
The shaded numbers are multiples of 10.

1	2	3	4	5	6	7	8	9	10
11	12	13	14	15	16	17	18	19	20
21	22	23	24	25	26	27	28	29	30
31	32	33	34	35	36	37	38	39	40
41	42	43	44	45	46	47	48	49	50
51	52	53	54	55	56	57	58	59	60
61	62	63	64	65	66	67	68	69	70
71	72	73	74	75	76	77	78	79	80
81	82	83	84	85	86	87	88	89	90
91	92	93	94	95	96	97	98	99	100

10, 20, 30 . . . 80, 90, 100.

How many groups of 10 are in 100?
What is the next multiple of 10 after 100?

Counting by Groups on the Number Line and 100 Chart

Can you use this number line to count by 2s? 10s?

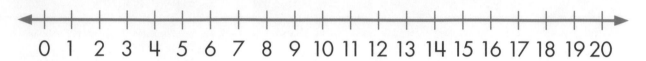

0 1 2 3 4 5 6 7 8 9 10 11 12 13 14 15 16 17 18 19 20

Can you use this 100 chart to count by 5s? By 10s?

1	2	3	4	5	6	7	8	9	10
11	12	13	14	15	16	17	18	19	20
21	22	23	24	25	26	27	28	29	30
31	32	33	34	35	36	37	38	39	40
41	42	43	44	45	46	47	48	49	50
51	52	53	54	55	56	57	58	59	60
61	62	63	64	65	66	67	68	69	70
71	72	73	74	75	76	77	78	79	80
81	82	83	84	85	86	87	88	89	90
91	92	93	94	95	96	97	98	99	100

Even and Odd Numbers

(page 1 of 2)

Math Words
- **even**
- **odd**

An even number can be divided into groups of 2.
An even number can be divided into 2 equal groups.

An even number of people can be put into pairs, with no one left over. An even number of people can make 2 equal teams.

| 10 people make 5 groups of 2 (partners). |  | 10 people make 2 groups of 5 (teams). |  |

10 is an even number.

An odd number cannot be divided into groups of 2.
An odd number cannot be divided into 2 equal groups.

An odd number of people cannot be put into pairs with no one left over. There is always one person left over. An odd number of people cannot make 2 equal teams. One team always has one more.

| 7 people make 3 groups of 2 (partners) with 1 person left over. |  | 7 people cannot make 2 equal teams. |  |

7 is an odd number.

 Is 11 even or odd? How do you know? What about 16?

Even and Odd Numbers

(page 2 of 2)

If you start at 0 and count by 2s, you say the even numbers.
If you start at 1 and count by 2s, you say the odd numbers.
On this 100 chart, the odd numbers are yellow.
The even numbers are green.

Odd and even numbers alternate in a pattern.

1	2	3	4	5	6	7	8	9	10
11	12	13	14	15	16	17	18	19	20
21	22	23	24	25	26	27	28	29	30
31	32	33	34	35	36	37	38	39	40
41	42	43	44	45	46	47	48	49	50
51	52	53	54	55	56	57	58	59	60
61	62	63	64	65	66	67	68	69	70
71	72	73	74	75	76	77	78	79	80
81	82	83	84	85	86	87	88	89	90
91	92	93	94	95	96	97	98	99	100

**Is 35 even or odd? How do you know?
What about 60? 101?**

Addition Combinations

One of your goals in math class this year is to practice and review all the addition combinations up to $10 + 10$.

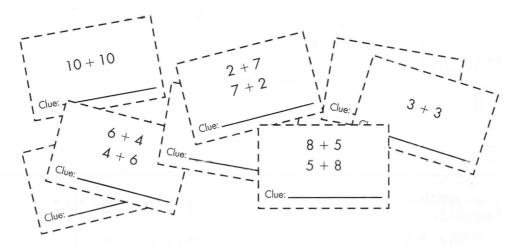

Learning Two Combinations at a Time

These two problems look different, but have the same answer.

8 + 3	3 + 8

When you know that $8 + 3 = 11$,
you also know that $3 + 8 = 11$.
You have learned two addition combinations.

Why do these two problems have the same answer?
$7 + 2 = 9$ $2 + 7 = 9$

Plus 1 Combinations

Any number plus 1 is a Plus 1 combination. So is 1 plus any number. Here are all of the Plus 1 combinations you are working on.

The Plus 1 Combinations

0 + 1 = 1		1 + 0 = 1
1 + 1 = 2		1 + 1 = 2
2 + 1 = 3		1 + 2 = 3
3 + 1 = 4		1 + 3 = 4
4 + 1 = 5		1 + 4 = 5
5 + 1 = 6		1 + 5 = 6
6 + 1 = 7		1 + 6 = 7
7 + 1 = 8		1 + 7 = 8
8 + 1 = 9		1 + 8 = 9
9 + 1 = 10		1 + 9 = 10
10 + 1 = 11		1 + 10 = 11

Do you notice a pattern in the Plus 1 combinations? Which ones do you know? Are there any you are still working on?

Plus 2 Combinations

Any number plus 2 is a Plus 2 combination. So is 2 plus any number. Here are all of the Plus 2 combinations you are working on.

The Plus 2 Combinations

$0 + 2 = 2$		$2 + 0 = 2$
$1 + 2 = 3$		$2 + 1 = 3$
$2 + 2 = 4$		$2 + 2 = 4$
$3 + 2 = 5$		$2 + 3 = 5$
$4 + 2 = 6$		$2 + 4 = 6$
$5 + 2 = 7$		$2 + 5 = 7$
$6 + 2 = 8$		$2 + 6 = 8$
$7 + 2 = 9$		$2 + 7 = 9$
$8 + 2 = 10$		$2 + 8 = 10$
$9 + 2 = 11$		$2 + 9 = 11$
$10 + 2 = 12$		$2 + 10 = 12$

Do you notice a pattern in the Plus 2 combinations? Which ones do you know? Are there any you are still working on?

Combinations of 10

Two numbers that add together to make 10 are a combination of 10.

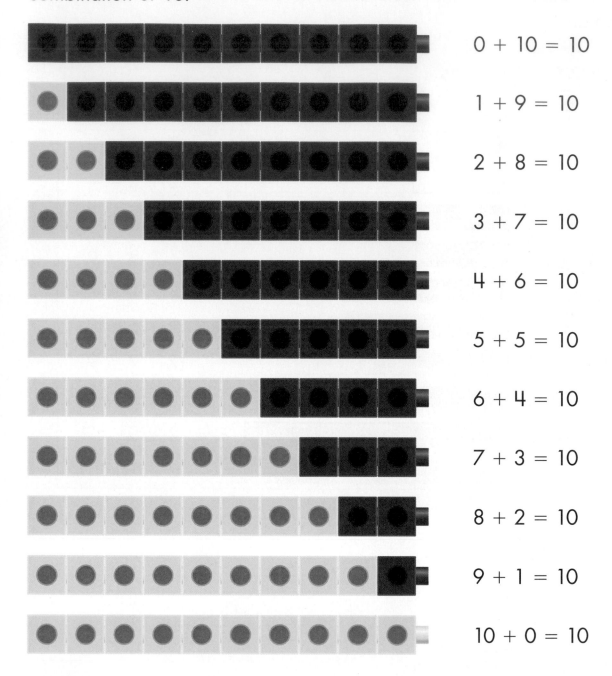

$0 + 10 = 10$

$1 + 9 = 10$

$2 + 8 = 10$

$3 + 7 = 10$

$4 + 6 = 10$

$5 + 5 = 10$

$6 + 4 = 10$

$7 + 3 = 10$

$8 + 2 = 10$

$9 + 1 = 10$

$10 + 0 = 10$

What do you notice about the combinations of 10?
Which do you know? Are there any you are still working on?

Doubles

Any number plus itself is a double.
Here are the doubles from 1 to 10.

1 + 1 = 2	2 + 2 = 4
3 + 3 = 6	4 + 4 = 8
5 + 5 = 10	6 + 6 = 12
7 + 7 = 14	8 + 8 = 16
9 + 9 = 18	10 + 10 = 20

Do you notice a pattern in the doubles?
Which ones do you know? Which are you still working on?

Near Doubles (page 1 of 3)

Near doubles are addition combinations that are related
to the doubles.

$$4 + 3 = 7$$

double $\longrightarrow$ $4 + 4 = 8$ $\quad$ near doubles

$$4 + 5 = 9$$

$4 + 3 = 7$ and $4 + 5 = 9$ are close to $4 + 4 = 8$.

You can use what you know about the doubles to learn
the near doubles.

If you know that $4 + 4 = 8$, you know that $4 + 3$ is 1 less
and $4 + 5$ is 1 more.

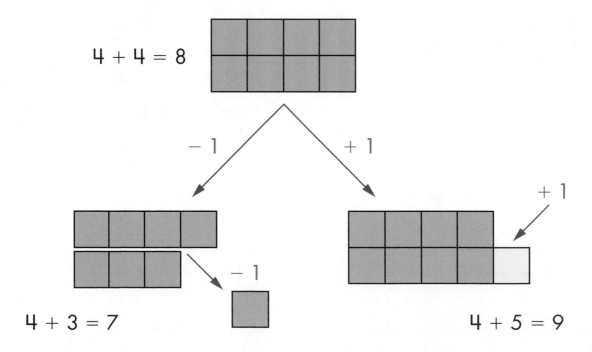

$4 + 4 = 8$

-1 $\qquad$ $+1$

$+1$

-1

$4 + 3 = 7$ $\qquad\qquad\qquad$ $4 + 5 = 9$

Near Doubles (page 2 of 3)

Here are the near doubles. Each is next to the double it is related to.

DOUBLE − 1	DOUBLE	DOUBLE + 1
1 + 0 = 1 Think: 1 + 1 − 1	1 + 1 = 2	1 + 2 = 3 Think: 1 + 1 + 1
2 + 1 = 3 Think: 2 + 2 − 1	2 + 2 = 4	2 + 3 = 5 Think: 2 + 2 + 1
3 + 2 = 5 Think: 3 + 3 − 1	3 + 3 = 6	3 + 4 = 7 Think: 3 + 3 + 1
4 + 3 = 7 Think: 4 + 4 − 1	4 + 4 = 8	4 + 5 = 9 Think: 4 + 4 + 1

Near Doubles (page 3 of 3)

DOUBLE − 1	DOUBLE	DOUBLE + 1
5 + 4 = 9 Think: 5 + 5 − 1	5 + 5 = 10	5 + 6 = 11 Think: 5 + 5 + 1
6 + 5 = 11 Think: 6 + 6 − 1	6 + 6 = 12	6 + 7 = 13 Think: 6 + 6 + 1
7 + 6 = 13 Think: 7 + 7 − 1	7 + 7 = 14	7 + 8 = 15 Think: 7 + 7 + 1
8 + 7 = 15 Think: 8 + 8 − 1	8 + 8 = 16	8 + 9 = 17 Think: 8 + 8 + 1

What addition combinations can 9 + 9 = 18 help you figure out? Which near doubles do you know? Which are you still working on?

Plus 10 Combinations

Any single-digit number plus 10 is a Plus 10 combination.
So is 10 plus any single-digit number. Here are all of the
Plus 10 combinations you are working on.

10 + 0 = 10 0 + 10 = 10	
10 + 1 = 11 1 + 10 = 11	
10 + 2 = 12 2 + 10 = 12	
10 + 3 = 13 3 + 10 = 13	
10 + 4 = 14 4 + 10 = 14	
10 + 5 = 15 5 + 10 = 15	
10 + 6 = 16 6 + 10 = 16	
10 + 7 = 17 7 + 10 = 17	
10 + 8 = 18 8 + 10 = 18	
10 + 9 = 19 9 + 10 = 19	

**What patterns do you notice in the Plus 10 combinations?
Which ones do you know? Which are you still working on?**

Plus 9 Combinations

Any number plus 9 is a Plus 9 combination. So is 9 plus any number. Here are the Plus 9 combinations you are working on.

9 + 1 = 10	9 + 2 = 11	9 + 3 = 12	9 + 4 = 13
1 + 9 = 10	2 + 9 = 11	3 + 9 = 12	4 + 9 = 13
9 + 5 = 14	9 + 6 = 15	9 + 7 = 16	9 + 8 = 17
5 + 9 = 14	6 + 9 = 15	7 + 9 = 16	8 + 9 = 17
9 + 9 = 18	9 + 10 = 19	10 + 9 = 19	

Some children learn the Plus 9 combinations by relating them to Plus 10 combinations they know.

9 + 6 = 15
6 + 9 = 15

Clue: 9 + 1 + 5 = 15

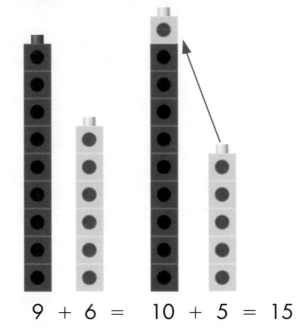

9 + 6 = 10 + 5 = 15

What helps you remember the Plus 9 combinations? Which ones do you know? Which are you still working on?

The Remaining Addition Combinations

You have learned these addition combinations so far.

Plus 1   Doubles
Plus 2   Near Doubles
Combinations of 10   Plus 10
                                Plus 9

Now there are just a few addition combinations left.
Here they are.

3 + 5	3 + 6	3 + 8	4 + 7	4 + 8	5 + 7	5 + 8	6 + 8
5 + 3	6 + 3	8 + 3	7 + 4	8 + 4	7 + 5	8 + 5	8 + 6

Here are some clues to help you remember 6 + 8 and 8 + 6.

Kira thinks about doubles.

"I know 6 + 6 = 12.
8 is 2 more than 6, so
6 + 8 is 2 more than
6 + 6. So, 6 + 8 is 14."

Jake uses 10.

"8 + 6 is the same
as 8 + 2, which is
10, plus 4 more.
The answer is 14."

**Which of these combinations are hard for you to remember?
Can you think of a clue to help you remember them?**

Number Strings

Number strings are addition problems with more than
2 numbers or addends. Using combinations you know
can help you solve these problems quickly and easily.
Here is an example.

$$6 + 4 + 6 = \underline{}$$

Leo uses a double.

"6 and 6 is 12.
Then 4 more is
13, 14, 15, 16."

Holly uses a combination of 10.

"6 + 4 = 10,
and
10 + 6 = 16."

Here's another example.

$$8 + 5 + 2 = \underline{}$$

Tia uses a combination of 10.

"8 and 2 is 10,
plus 5 more
is 15."

Roshaun uses
a near double.

"5 and 2 is 7.
So then I've got
8 + 7. I know
7 + 7 = 14, so
8 + 7 = 15."

How would you solve 7 + 4 + 7 + 6 + 3?
What combinations would you start with?

Today's Number

Today's Number is 18.

Here are some different ways to make 18.

10 + 8 = 18	4 + 4 + 4 + 4 + 2 = 18
20 − 2 = 18	18 = 100 − 82
18 = 9 + 9	15 + 15 − 12 = 18

What are some more ways to make 18?

Today's Number:
Addition Combinations

When you make Today's Number, sometimes there are rules to follow. For example:

Today's Number is 26.

Here are some ways to make 26 with Combinations of 10 or Doubles Combinations.

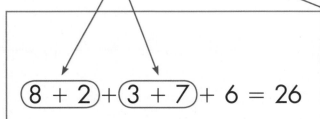

$(8 + 2) + (3 + 7) + 6 = 26$	$26 = (10 + 10) + 6$
$26 = 9 + 1 + 6 + 4 + 6$	$15 + 15 - 4 = 26$
$30 - 4 = 26$	$26 = 9 + 9 + 4 + 4$

What are other ways to make 26 with doubles? with combinations of 10? with both?

Today's Number: Coin Values

Today's Number is 56.

Here are some ways to make 56 with coin values.

25 + 25 + 5 + 1 = 56

10 + 10 + 10 + 10 + 10 + 5 + 1 = 56

5 + 5 + 10 + 10 + 25 + 1 = 56

25 + 25 + 1 + 1 + 1 + 1 + 1 + 1 = 56

 What are ways to make 56 with coins?

Today's Number: Tens and Ones

Today's Number is 72.

Here are some ways to make 72 with tens and ones.

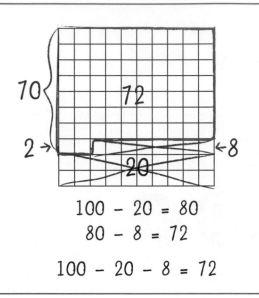

$$100 - 20 = 80$$
$$80 - 8 = 72$$
$$100 - 20 - 8 = 72$$

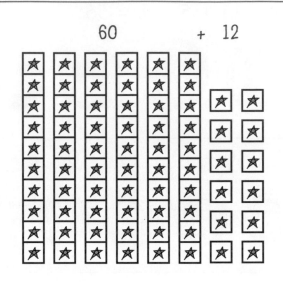

60   +   12

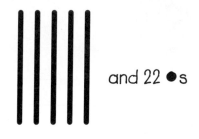

and 22 ●s

$$50 \quad + \quad 22 \quad = \quad 72$$

$$10 + 10 + 10 + 10 + 10 + 10 + 10 + 2 = 72$$

What are other ways to make 72 with tens and ones?

An Addition Story Problem

Here is a story problem.

Sally has 10 crayons. Jake gave her 12 more crayons.
How many crayons does Sally have now?

In this problem, two groups are being combined or joined.
This equation shows what is happening in this problem.

$$10 + 12 = \underline{\quad ? \quad}$$

Does Sally have more crayons at the beginning of the story or at the end?

Solving An Addition Story Problem

Here is the story.

Sally has 10 crayons. Jake gave her 12 more crayons.
How many crayons does Sally have now?

There are many ways to solve this problem.
Here is what some students did.

Jake counted on from 10.

$10 + 12 = \underline{22}$

11 12 13 14 15 16

17 18 19 20 21 22

Sally used what she knew about addition combinations.

I know
10 + 10 = 20,
so
10 + 12 = 22.

Leigh split 12 into 10 and 2. Then she used the number line to add.

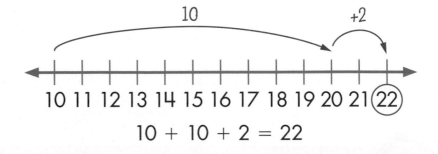

$10 + 10 + 2 = 22$

How would you solve this problem?

Addition Notation

Sally has 10 crayons. Jake gave her 12 more crayons. Now Sally has 22 crayons.

Here are 2 equations for this problem.

$$10 + 12 = 22$$

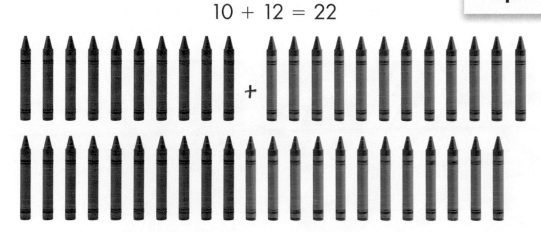

10 plus 12 is equal to 22.

$$22 = 10 + 12$$

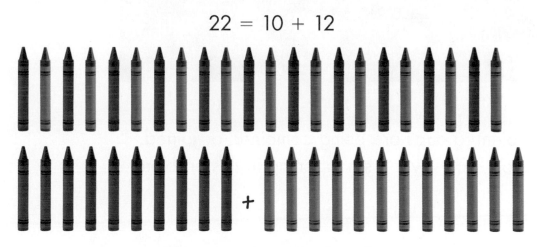

22 is equal to 10 plus 12.

10 and 12 are the addends. 22 is the total or sum.
The equal sign shows that 10 + 12 is the same amount as 22.

What is the same and what is different about these two equations?

Another Addition Story Problem

Here is another story problem.

Sally went to Sticker Station. She bought 42 moon stickers and 35 star stickers. How many stickers did Sally buy?

In this problem, groups are being combined or joined. This equation shows what is happening in this problem.

$$42 + 35 = \underline{\hphantom{00}}$$

How many strips of 10 did Sally have?
How many singles? How many stickers altogether?

Solving Another Addition Story Problem (page 1 of 2)

Here is the story.

Sally went to Sticker Station. She bought 42 moon stickers and 35 star stickers. How many stickers did Sally buy?

There are many ways to solve this problem.

Some children think about tens and ones.

Chen used strips and singles to show the stickers Sally bought.

$$42 + 35 = \underline{}$$

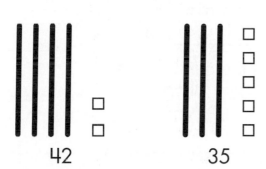

He put the tens together and the ones together.

7 strips of 10 is 70.   7 singles is 7.

Then he added. 70 + 7 = 77.
Sally bought 77 stickers.

Holly and Simon broke both numbers into tens and ones. They added the tens first, and then the ones.

Holly recorded like this:

$$35 + 42 = \underline{}$$
$$30 + 40 = 70$$
$$5 + 2 = 7$$
$$70 + 7 = 77$$

Simon recorded like this:

$$\begin{array}{r} 35 \\ + \ 42 \\ \hline 70 \\ + \ 7 \\ \hline 77 \end{array}$$

Solving Another Addition Story Problem (page 2 of 2)

Other children keep one number whole and add the other number on in parts.

Henry thought about stickers.

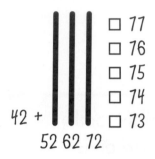

42 +
52 62 72

☐ 77
☐ 76
☐ 75
☐ 74
☐ 73

Carla used the 100 chart. She added 35 stickers onto the 42 Sally already had.

1	2	3	4	5	6	7	8	9	10
11	12	13	14	15	16	17	18	19	20
21	22	23	24	25	26	27	28	29	30
31	32	33	34	35	36	37	38	39	40
41	42	43	44	45	46	47	48	49	50
51	52	53	54	55	56	57	58	59	60
61	62	63	64	65	66	67	68	69	70
71	72	73	74	75	76	77	78	79	80
81	82	83	84	85	86	87	88	89	90
91	92	93	94	95	96	97	98	99	100

+ 8
+10
+10
+ 2 + 5

$$\begin{array}{r} 42 \\ + 35 \\ \hline 77 \end{array}$$

Jeffrey started at 42 and added on 35 on the number line.

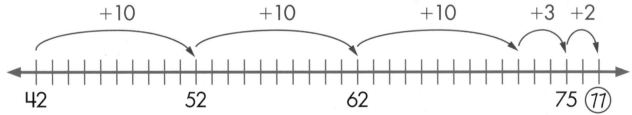

+10   +10   +10   +3 +2

42   52   62   75 (77)

Simon broke 35 into 30 and 5 to add it onto 42.

42 + 35 = ___
42 + 30 = 72
72 + 5 = 77
77 stickers

Leo kept the 35 whole. He added the 42 by adding 40 and then 2 more.

35 + 42 = ___

$$\begin{array}{r} 35 \\ + 40 \\ \hline 75 \\ + 2 \\ \hline 77 \end{array}$$

Tia solved this problem by adding 40 + 37. What did she do? Why does that work?

Solving an Addition Problem
(page 1 of 2)

Here is another problem.

$$38 + 23 = \underline{\hphantom{00}}$$

$$\begin{array}{r} 38 \\ + \ 23 \\ \hline \end{array}$$

There are many ways to solve this problem.

These children broke both numbers into tens and ones. They added the tens together and the ones together, and then added those totals.

Juan used stickers.

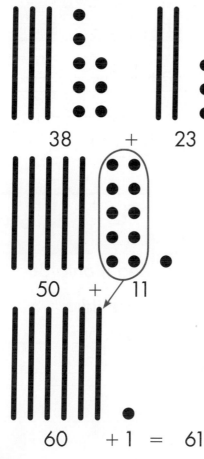

38   +   23

$30 + 20 = 50$

$8 + 3 = 11$

50   +   11

$50 + 10 = 60$

$60 + 1 = 61$

60   + 1   =   61

Monisha's Solution

$$38 + 23 = \underline{\hphantom{00}}$$
$$30 + 20 = 50$$
$$8 + 3 = 11$$
$$50 + 11 = 61$$

Travis' Solution

$$\begin{array}{r} 38 \\ + \ 23 \\ \hline 50 \\ + \ 11 \\ \hline 61 \end{array}$$

If there are 3 tens in 38 and 2 tens in 23, why is the answer in the 60s instead of in the 50s?

Solving an Addition Problem
(page 2 of 2)

These children keep one number whole and add the other number on in parts.

| Amaya thought about stickers. | Luis used the 100 chart. |

Amaya thought about stickers.

$38 + 23 = \underline{61}$

38 +

    48 58

☐ 59
☐ 60
☐ 61

Luis used the 100 chart.

$38 + 23 = \underline{\hphantom{00}}$

1	2	3	4	5	6	7	8	9	10
11	12	13	14	15	16	17	18	19	20
21	22	23	24	25	26	27	28	29	30
31	32	33	34	35	36	37	**38**	39	40
41	42	43	44	45	46	47	48	49	50
51	52	53	54	55	56	57	58	59	60
61	62	63	64	65	66	67	68	69	70
71	72	73	74	75	76	77	78	79	80
81	82	83	84	85	86	87	88	89	90
91	92	93	94	95	96	97	98	99	100

+20
+ 3

Jacy started at 38 and added on 23 on the number line.

$38 + 23 = \underline{\hphantom{00}}$

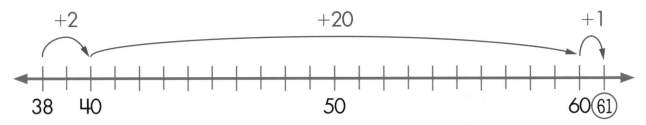

+2   +20   +1

38   40   50   60 ⑥61

Leo and Nate broke 23 into 20 and 3 and then added it onto 38.

| Leo recorded like this: | Nate recorded like this: |

Leo recorded like this:

$38 + 23 = \underline{61}$
$38 + 20 = 58$
$58 + 3 = 61$

Nate recorded like this:

$38 + 23 = \underline{\hphantom{00}}$

$$\begin{array}{r} 38 \\ + 20 \\ \hline 58 \\ + 3 \\ \hline 61 \end{array}$$

Esteban solved this problem by adding 40 + 21. What did he do? Why does that work?

A Subtraction Story Problem

Here is a story problem.

Carla had 16 shells. She gave 7 of them to Juanita.
How many shells did Carla have left?

In this problem, Carla starts with a group of shells and
gives some away.

This equation shows what is happening in this problem.

$$16 - 7 = \underline{\ \ \ }$$

**Does Carla have more shells at the beginning of the story
or at the end?**

Solving a Subtraction Story Problem

Here is the story.

Carla had 16 shells. She gave 7 of them to Juanita.
How many shells did Carla have left?

There are many ways to solve this problem.
Here is what some students did.

Yama broke apart 7 into 6 and 1 and then subtracted from 16. 16 − 7 = ___ 16 − 6 = 10 10 − 1 = 9 So, 16 − 7 = 9.	Gregory used a number line and counted back 7. He got to 9. 16 − 7 = ___ 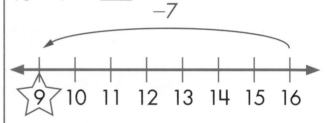

Katrina drew 16 shells and crossed out 7. There were 9 left.

16 − 7 = ___

Malcolm used an addition combination he knew.

The problem is asking 7 + ___ = 16.
I know 7 + _10_ = 17,
so 7 + _9_ = 16.
If 7 + 9 = 16,
then 16 − 7 = 9.

 How would you solve this problem?

Subtraction Notation

Math Words
• **minus**
• **difference**

Carla had 16 shells. She gave 7 of them to Juanita. Then Carla had 9 shells left.

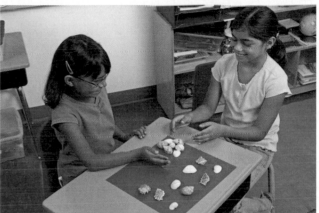

Here are two equations for this problem.

$$16 - 7 = 9$$

16 minus 7 is equal to 9.

$$9 = 16 - 7$$

9 equals 16 minus 7.

The difference between 16 and 7 is 9.

The equal sign shows that $16 - 7$ is the same amount as 9.

What is the same and what is different about these two equations?

Another Subtraction Story Problem

Travis had 48 circus stickers. He gave 22 to Nadia. How many circus stickers does Travis have left?

In this problem, Travis starts with 48 stickers. He gives 22 to Nadia.

This equation shows what is happening in this problem.

$$48 - 22 = \underline{\hphantom{00}}$$

Does Travis have more stickers at the beginning of the story or at the end?

Solving Another Subtraction Story Problem (page 1 of 2)

Here is the story.

Travis had 48 circus stickers. He gave 22 to Nadia.
How many circus stickers does Travis have left?

There are many ways to solve this problem.
Some children show 48 stickers. Then they remove
or cross out 22 of them, and count how many are left.

Leigh drew 48 stickers, crossed out 22, and counted how many were left. 48 − 22 = ___  10 20 and 6 more is 26 She has 26 stickers left.	Gregory broke up the 48 so he could subtract 22. 48 = 20 + ~~20~~ + 6 + ~~2~~ 26 are left!

Other children subtract 22 from 48 in parts.

Jacy used a number line to subtract 22 from 48. 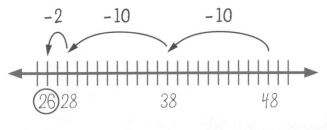 48 − 22 = 26	Malcolm broke 22 into 20 and 2. First he subtracted 20, then he subtracted 2. 48 − 22 = ? 48 − 20 = 28 28 − 2 = 26

Solving Another Subtraction Story Problem (page 2 of 2)

Other children think, "22 + ___ = 48." They think about how much they have to add to 22 to get to 48.

Roshaun used a number line.

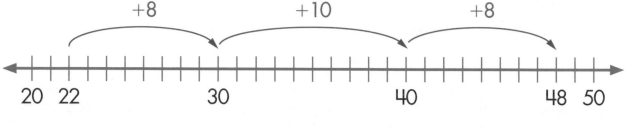

$$22 + 26 = 48$$

Travis used the 100 chart.

1	2	3	4	5	6	7	8	9	10
11	12	13	14	15	16	17	18	19	20
21	22	23	24	25	26	27	28	29	30
31	32	33	34	35	36	37	38	39	40
41	42	43	44	45	46	47	48	49	50
51	52	53	54	55	56	57	58	59	60
61	62	63	64	65	66	67	68	69	70
71	72	73	74	75	76	77	78	79	80
81	82	83	84	85	86	87	88	89	90
91	92	93	94	95	96	97	98	99	100

$$\begin{array}{r} 8 \\ 10 \\ + 8 \\ \hline 26 \end{array}$$

Paige used equations to record her thinking.

$$22 + \underline{26} = 48$$
$$22 + \underline{20} = 42$$
$$42 + \underline{6} = 48$$
$$20 + \underline{6} = 26$$

 How would you solve this problem?

Solving a Subtraction Problem

(page 1 of 3)

Here is another problem.   72 − 38 = ___

$$\begin{array}{r} 72 \\ - \ 38 \\ \hline \end{array}$$

There are many ways to solve this problem.

Some children show 72 stickers. Then they remove
or cross out 38 of them, and count how many are left.

Amaya drew 72 stickers.

To cross out 38, she had to
change one strip to singles.

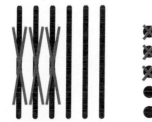

She counted how many were left.
"10, 20, 30, and 4 more is 34."

Carla used the 100 chart.

1	2	3	4	5	6	7	8	9	10	
11	12	13	14	15	16	17	18	19	20	
21	22	23	24	25	26	27	28	29	30	
31	32	33	34	35	36	37	38	39	40	+ 2
41	42	43	44	45	46	47	48	49	50	+10
51	52	53	54	55	56	57	58	59	60	+10
61	62	63	64	65	66	67	68	69	70	+10
71	72	73	74	75	76	77	78	79	80	+ 2
81	82	83	84	85	86	87	88	89	90	34
91	92	93	94	95	96	97	98	99	100	

72 − 38 = 34

Henry thought:

> You can
> break 72 into
> 40 + 30 + 2.
> If you take the 38
> away from the 40,
> there's 2 left.
> 2 + 30 + 2 = 34.

Roshaun drew 72 stickers, crossed out
38, and counted how many were left.

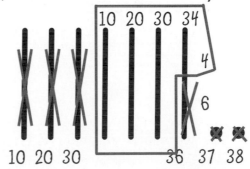

Solving a Subtraction Problem

(page 2 of 3)

Other children subtract 38 from 72 in parts.

Tia used the 100 chart. She started at 72 and counted back 38. She subtracted 2 first, then 30, then 6 more. 34 were left.

$72 - 38 = 34$

1	2	3	4	5	6	7	8	9	10
11	12	13	14	15	16	17	18	19	20
21	22	23	24	25	26	27	28	29	30
31	32	33	34	35	36	37	38	39	40
41	42	43	44	45	46	47	48	49	50
51	52	53	54	55	56	57	58	59	60
61	62	63	64	65	66	67	68	69	70
71	72	73	74	75	76	77	78	79	80
81	82	83	84	85	86	87	88	89	90
91	92	93	94	95	96	97	98	99	100

-6 -30 -2

Melissa used the same strategy as Tia, but she used the number line to subtract in parts. She subtracted 2 first, then 30, then 6 more.

$72 - 38 =$ ___

$72 - 2 = 70$
$70 - 30 = 40$
$40 - 6 = 34$

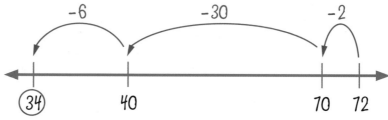

Alberto broke 38 into 30 and 8. First he subtracted the 30. Then he subtracted the 8.

$$72 - 30 = 42$$
$$42 - 8 = 34$$
$$72 - 38 = \underline{34}$$

Solving a Subtraction Problem

(page 3 of 3)

To solve 72 − 38, other children think, "38 + ___ = 72."
They think about how much they have to add to 38 to get
to 72.

Anita used the 100 chart
to add up.

10 + 10 + 10 + 4 = 34

1	2	3	4	5	6	7	8	9	10
11	12	13	14	15	16	17	18	19	20
21	22	23	24	25	26	27	28	29	30
31	32	33	34	35	36	37	**38**	39	40
41	42	43	44	45	46	47	48	49	50
51	52	53	54	55	56	57	58	59	60
61	62	63	64	65	66	67	68	69	70
71	72	73	74	75	76	77	78	79	80
81	82	83	84	85	86	87	88	89	90
91	92	93	94	95	96	97	98	99	100

Henry kept adding 10 until he got close to 72.

$$38 + 10 = 48$$
$$48 + 10 = 58$$
$$58 + 10 = 68$$
$$68 + 4 = 72$$

10 + 10 + 10 + 4 = 34

Lonzell used the number line to add up.

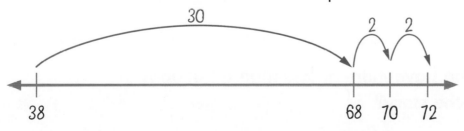

30 + 2 + 2 = 34

How Many More? (page 1 of 5)

Here is another story problem.

Katrina had 8 balloons. Then she got some more. When she recounted, she had 11 balloons. How many more did she get?

In this problem, Katrina starts with a group of 8 balloons.

She gets some more.
Then she has 11.

You need to figure out how many more she gets.

These equations can go with this story problem.

$8 + \underline{\quad} = 11$

$11 - \underline{\quad} = 8$

$11 = 8 + \underline{\quad}$

$11 - 8 = \underline{\quad}$

Does Katrina have more or less than 8 balloons at the end of the story?

How Many More? (page 2 of 5)

Katrina had 8 balloons. Then she got some more. When she recounted, she had 11 balloons. How many did she get?

There are many ways to solve this problem. This is what some children did.

Anita counted up from 8 until she got to 11 on a number line.

$8 + \underline{\quad} = 11$

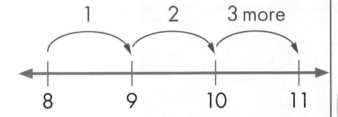

She got 3 more.

Malcolm counted down from 11.

$11 - \underline{\quad} = 8$

If Katrina had 11 at the end . . . 1 less is 10, 2 less is 9, 3 less is 8. She got 3 more balloons.

Juan drew the 11 balloons Katrina had at the end of the story. He drew a box around the 8 and counted the others.

$11 - 8 = \underline{\quad}$

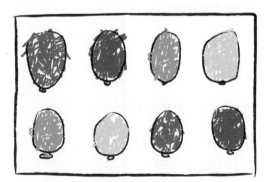

Katrina started with 8 balloons.

She got 3 more.

 How would you solve this problem?

How Many More? (page 3 of 5)

You can use what you know about combinations of 10 and multiples of 10 to solve addition or subtraction problems. For example, if you have 46 cubes and need 70:

$$46 + \underline{\quad} = 70$$

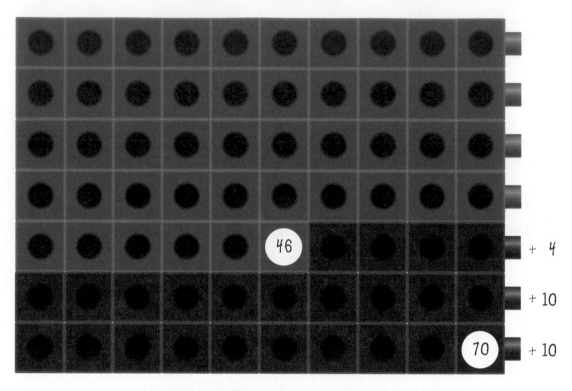

+ 4
+ 10
+ 10

Putting it together

$$46 + 4 = 50$$
$$50 + 10 = 60$$
$$60 + 10 = 70$$

$$4 + 10 + 10 = 24$$
So, $46 + \mathbf{24} = 70$.

If I have 35 marbles, how many more do I need to get 60?
If I have 58 stickers, how many more do I need to get 90?

How Many More? (page 4 of 5)

If you have 81 pennies, how many more to 100?

81 + ___ = 100

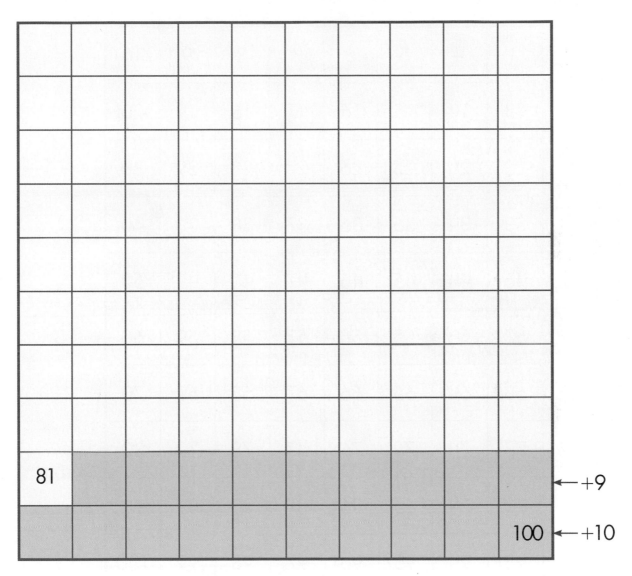

81

←—+9

100 ←—+10

81 + __19__ = 100

How Many More? (page 5 of 5)

Find 57 on the 100 chart. How many more to 100?

57 + ___ = 100

1	2	3	4	5	6	7	8	9	10
11	12	13	14	15	16	17	18	19	20
21	22	23	24	25	26	27	28	29	30
31	32	33	34	35	36	37	38	39	40
41	42	43	44	45	46	47	48	49	50
51	52	53	54	55	56	57	58	59	60
61	62	63	64	65	66	67	68	69	70
71	72	73	74	75	76	77	78	79	80
81	82	83	84	85	86	87	88	89	90
91	92	93	94	95	96	97	98	99	100

←—+3

+40

57 + **43** = 100

If you have 44, how many more do you need to get 100?
How far is it from 72 to 100?

Math Symbols

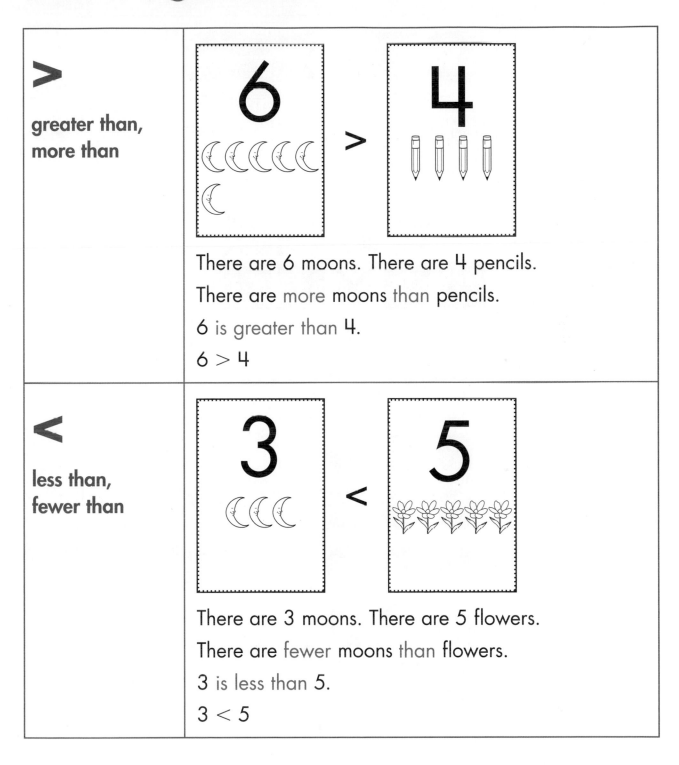

>

greater than, more than

There are 6 moons. There are 4 pencils.

There are more moons than pencils.

6 is greater than 4.

6 > 4

<

less than, fewer than

There are 3 moons. There are 5 flowers.

There are fewer moons than flowers.

3 is less than 5.

3 < 5

Using Math Symbols (page 1 of 2)

+ plus sign addition sign	 4 + 6 = 10 4 plus 6 is equal to 10. 4 plus 6 equals 10.
— minus sign subtraction sign	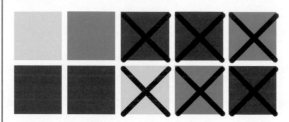 10 − 6 = 4 10 minus 6 is equal to 4. 10 minus 6 equals 4.
= equal sign	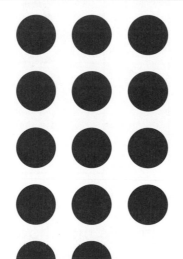 =  14 = 14 14 is the same as 14. 14 is equal to 14. 14 equals 14.

Using Math Symbols (page 2 of 2)

An equation uses numbers and symbols to show what is happening in a math problem.

$$10 + 14 = 24$$

$$24 - 14 = 10$$

Here are two ways to write addition problems.

$$\begin{array}{r} 10 \\ + 14 \\ \hline 24 \end{array}$$ is the same as $10 + 14 = 24$

Here are two ways to write subtraction problems.

$24 - 14 = 10$ is the same as $$\begin{array}{r} 24 \\ - 14 \\ \hline 10 \end{array}$$

Fractions

Fractions are equal parts of a whole.

Fractions show how many parts in a whole and how many of those parts you have.

Here is a sandwich cut into equal parts.

The sandwich is cut in half because there are two equal pieces.

If you eat one of those pieces, you will eat one half of a sandwich.

Here are some other ways to divide this sandwich in half.

Writing Fractions

All fractions are written with two numbers. There is always a line between the two numbers. The line can be straight or slanted.

For example, you can write the fraction "one half" as $\frac{1}{2}$ or $\frac{1}{2}$.

The bottom number shows how many equal pieces are in the whole. The sandwich was cut into 2 equal pieces.

$\frac{1}{2}$

The top number shows how many pieces of the sandwich Juan is taking.

 What else can be divided into two equal parts?

One Half

$\frac{1}{2}$ is one of two equal parts.

This sandwich is cut in half.

This orange is cut in half.

Half of 10¢ is 5¢.

$\frac{1}{2}$ of this flag is red.

$\frac{1}{2}$ of this flag is blue.

If you have 8 balloons and half float away, how many balloons do you have left?

One Fourth

Math Words
• **fourth**

$\frac{1}{4}$ is one of four equal parts.

This sandwich is cut
into fourths.

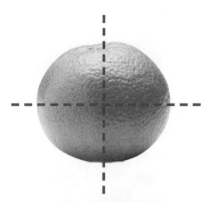

This orange is cut into fourths.

One fourth of 12¢ is 3¢.

$\frac{1}{4}$ of this flag is blue.

**If you had 8 balloons and one fourth floated away,
how many balloons floated away?**

Two Fourths

$\frac{2}{4}$ is two of four equal parts. Two fourths is the same amount as one half ($\frac{1}{2}$).

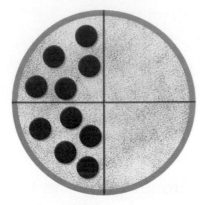

$\frac{2}{4}$ of this pizza
has a topping.

Two fourths of the cans are red.

Two fourths of 12¢ is 6¢.

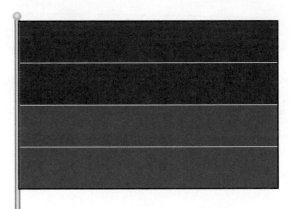

$\frac{2}{4}$ of this flag is blue.

If you had 8 balloons and two fourths floated away, how many balloons floated away?

Three Fourths

$\frac{3}{4}$ is three of four equal parts.

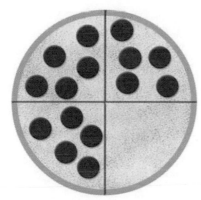

$\frac{3}{4}$ of this pizza
has a topping.

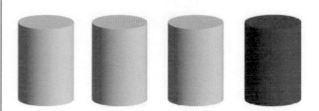

Three fourths of the cans
are yellow.

Three fourths of 12¢ is 9¢.

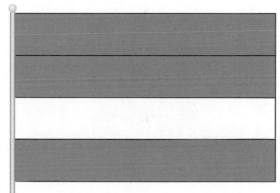

$\frac{3}{4}$ of this flag is green.

If you had 16 balloons and three fourths floated away, how many balloons floated away?

One Third

Math Words
- **third**

$\frac{1}{3}$ is one of three equal parts.

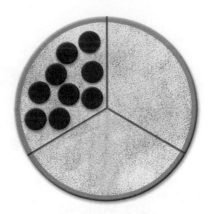

One third of this pizza has a topping.

$\frac{1}{3}$ of this cup is filled with juice.

$\frac{1}{3}$ of the balloons are orange.

One third of this flag is red.
One third is white.
One third is blue.

 How many is $\frac{1}{3}$ of nine pennies?

Two Thirds

$\frac{2}{3}$ is two of three equal parts.

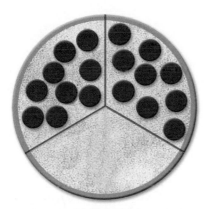

Two thirds of this pizza has a topping.

$\frac{2}{3}$ of this cup is filled with juice.

$\frac{2}{3}$ of the balloons are yellow.

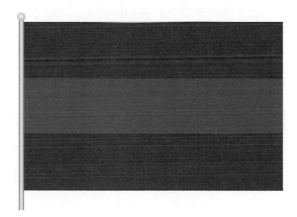

Two thirds of this flag is red.

If you have 9 pennies and spend two thirds of them, how many did you spend? How many pennies will you have left?

Mixed Numbers

Mixed numbers are whole numbers and fractions together.

Math Words
- mixed number

$2\frac{1}{4}$

$3\frac{1}{2}$

$5\frac{2}{3}$

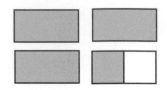

$2\frac{1}{4}$ is between 2 and 3. | $3\frac{1}{2}$ is between 3 and 4. | $5\frac{2}{3}$ is between 5 and 6.

There are many times to use mixed numbers.

Paige is $4\frac{1}{2}$ feet tall. She measures 4 whole feet and $\frac{1}{2}$ of another foot.

If four children share 6 sandwiches, each child gets 1 whole sandwich and half a sandwich.

When do you use mixed numbers?

A Growing Pattern

Math Words
• **pattern**

Look at this example about a group of people and the number of eyes.

1 person
2 eyes

2 people
4 eyes

3 people
6 eyes

4 people
8 eyes

Every time one more person joins the group, the total number of eyes goes up by 2.

Understanding how a pattern grows and changes can help you figure out what will come next.

What is the total number of eyes for 5 people?

Tables (page 1 of 2)

A table is a way to organize information.

A table is made up of columns going up and down and rows going across. Look at this table about people and eyes.

Columns go up and down.

Number of People	Total Number of Eyes
1 person	2 eyes
2 people	4 eyes
3 people	6 eyes
4 people	8 eyes
5 people	10 eyes
6 people	12 eyes
7 people	14 eyes

Rows go across.

Tables (page 2 of 2)

Here is the same table with only numbers. See if you can figure out what each row and column is showing.

This row shows that 2 people have a total of 4 eyes.

Number of People	Total Number of Eyes
1	2
2	4
3	6
4	8
5	10
6	12
7	14

This row shows that 4 people have a total of 8 eyes.

Do you see a pattern in this table?
What is the total number of eyes for 10 people?

Another Growing Pattern

This building is being built. Each floor of this building has 5 rooms.

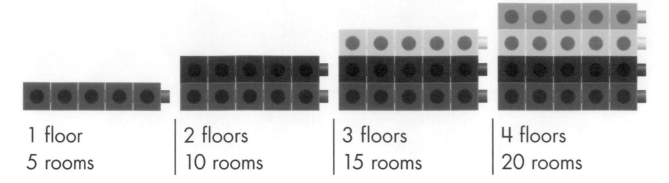

1 floor	2 floors	3 floors	4 floors
5 rooms	10 rooms	15 rooms	20 rooms

There are many ways to describe this growing pattern.

The building looks like a plus five pattern.

It grows by 5 each time.

How would you describe this pattern? What would the total numbers of rooms be if the building had 6 floors?

A Table for a Cube Building (page 1 of 2)

Total Number of Floors	Total Number of Rooms
1	5
2	10
3	15
4	20
5	25

This row shows that a building with 2 floors has 10 rooms.

10	?

This row shows 10 floors.

Here is a gap in the table. Floors 6, 7, 8, and 9 are not shown.

The gap in the table shows a jump from 5 floors to 10 floors. You can still think about 6 floors, 7 floors, 8 floors, and 9 floors to help you continue the pattern.

Can you figure out how many total rooms there would be in 10 floors of this building?

A Table for a Cube Building (page 2 of 2)

Can you figure out how many total rooms there would be on 10 floors of this building?

Several students thought about this problem and figured it out in different ways.

Leo counted by 5s ten times.

50
45
40
35
30
25
20
15
10
5

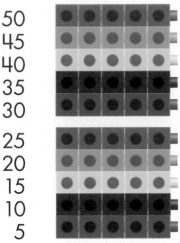

Melissa doubled the number of rooms on 5 floors.

I know 5 floors has 25 rooms. So, 10 floors must have twice as many rooms. 25 + 25 = 50. There are 50 rooms in 10 floors.

Simon counted on from 25 by 5s.

+5

25

30   35   40   45   50

Anita counted on 5 more floors by 1s.

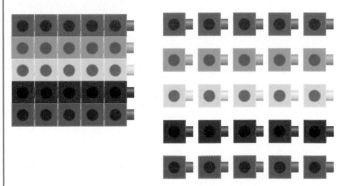

? How would you solve this problem?

Pattern Block Shapes

Here are the pattern block shapes.

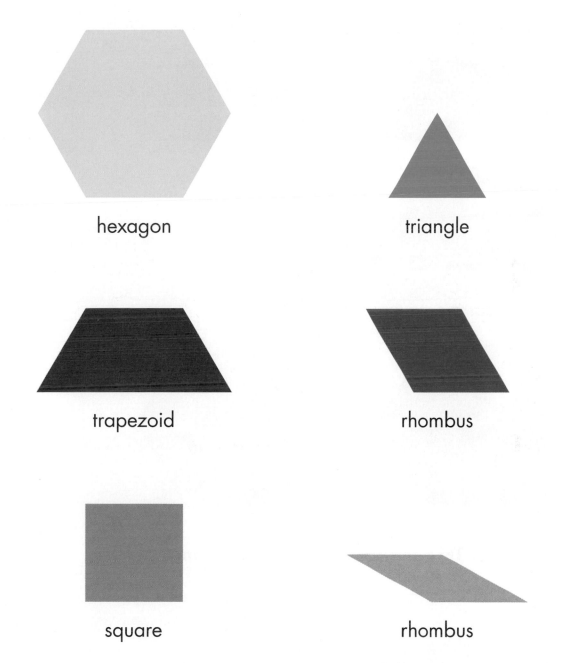

hexagon

triangle

trapezoid

rhombus

square

rhombus

A Growing Pattern with Pattern Blocks

One trapezoid can be covered by 3 triangles.

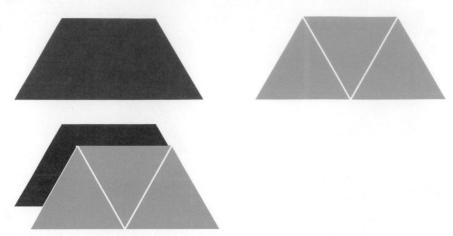

2 trapezoids can be covered by 6 triangles.

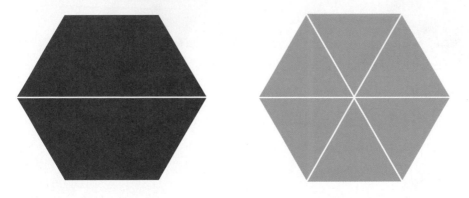

Number of Trapezoids	Number of Triangles
1	3
2	6
3	?

 How many triangles would cover 3 trapezoids?

Repeating Patterns

There are many examples of repeating patterns.
Here are a few.

- numbers

1 2 3 1 2 3 1 2 3 1 2 3 1 2 3

- colors

- shapes

- actions

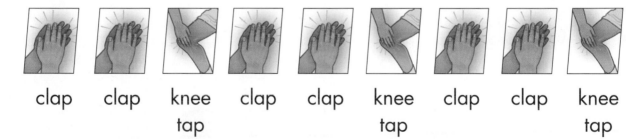

| clap | clap | knee tap | clap | clap | knee tap | clap | clap | knee tap |

 Is this a repeating pattern?

Unit

The unit is the part of the pattern that repeats over and over.

unit:

pattern:

unit: 1 2 3

pattern: 1 2 3 1 2 3 1 2 3 1 2 3 1 2 3

unit:

pattern:

Can you find the unit of this pattern?

Repeating Patterns on a Number Strip

A number strip can help record a repeating pattern.

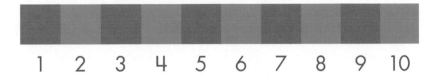

| 1 | 2 | 3 | 4 | 5 | 6 | 7 | 8 | 9 | 10 |

In this repeating pattern, each square is numbered.

The 1st square is green.

The 2nd square is blue.

The 3rd square is green.

The 4th square is blue.

The 5th square is green.

The 6th square is blue.

The 7th square is green.

The 8th square is blue.

The 9th square is green.

The 10th square is blue.

When a pattern repeats, you can use what you know to predict what will come next.

If this pattern keeps repeating in the same way, what color will go in the 12th square? Will the 15th square be blue or green? If the pattern repeats for 20 squares, how many squares will be blue?

Data

The information you collect is called data. One way to collect data is by asking a group of people the same question.

For example, Ms. Williams was planning an after-school program for second graders. She started by collecting data.

Ms. Williams collected the data to find out what second graders like to do after school.

Here is Ms. Williams's question.

> What is your favorite activity to do after school?

Ms. Williams will use the data she collects to help her decide what activities to offer.

What are some questions you have collected data about in your class?

Survey

Math Words
• survey

Doing a survey is a way to collect data. You conduct a survey by asking a group of people the same question and keeping track of their answers.

Here is Ms. Williams's after-school survey with the answers given by students.

What is your favorite activity to do after school?			
Student	**Favorite Activity**	**Student**	**Favorite Activity**
Alberto	Draw	**Jacy**	Play soccer
Anita	Check out books	**Leigh**	Play the piano
Carla	Play tag	**Leo**	Go to the playground
Carolina	Paint	**Nate**	Sew
Chen	Read stories and act out plays	**Malcolm**	Draw
Esteban	Listen to music	**Gregory**	Pretend
Henry	Play sports	**Rochelle**	Read stories and make up puppet shows
Holly	Dress up and act out plays	**Simon**	Play the drums
Jeffrey	T-ball	**Yama**	Go to the playground

Making Categories (page 1 of 2)

Putting data into categories can help you learn something about the group you surveyed.

Ms. Williams got many different responses from the students. She put them into categories to figure out which after-school classes to offer.

After looking at the data closely, Ms. Williams noticed that many of the students liked to do art activities. She decided to make one after-school class for these students.

ART CLASS	
Student	**Favorite Activity**
Alberto	Draw
Carolina	Paint
Nate	Sew
Malcolm	Draw

Look at the data on page 105.
What other categories could Ms. Williams make?
What other classes should be held?

Making Categories (page 2 of 2)

Ms. Williams looked at all the students' answers and put similar answers together. Making categories helped her figure out which after-school classes were needed.

Here are the categories.

Kind of Class	Students' Answers
Art	Draw, paint, sew, draw
Sports and outdoor play	Play tag, play sports, T-ball, play soccer, go to the playground, go to the playground
Pretend play	Pretend, dress up and act out plays, read stories and make up puppet shows
Music	Listen to music, play the piano, play the drums
Library	Check out books, read stories and act out plays, dress up and act out plays, read stories and make up puppet shows

Some of the answers in Pretend play and Library are the same.

What activities appear in both Pretend play and Library?

Venn Diagrams

Ms. Williams thought the students would be happy with the classes, but there was a problem. There were 5 classes, but only 4 teachers. What could she do?

Ms. Williams looked at the data again. She noticed that some of the activities were very similar. Students in the Pretend play category liked to read stories and act out plays, and so did students in the Library category. She made a Venn diagram to help her think about this.

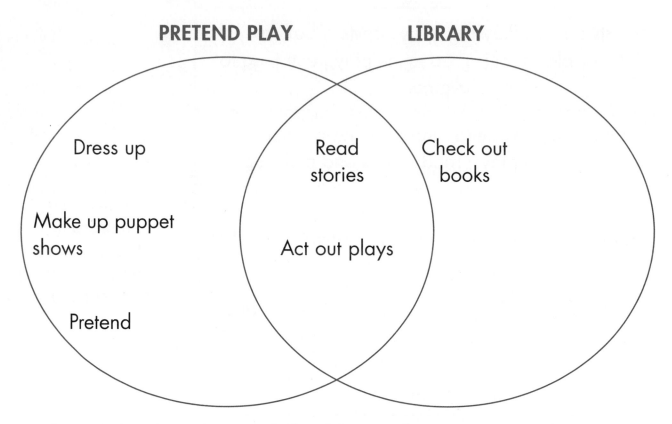

PRETEND PLAY   **LIBRARY**

Dress up

Make up puppet shows

Pretend

Read stories

Act out plays

Check out books

Looking at the Venn diagram helped Ms. Williams see that there was some overlap between the two classes. She decided to join the classes so that all the students in Pretend play and Library could read and act out stories and plays. The new after-school class was called Drama.

Organizing the Data

It was time for Ms. Williams to figure out which rooms to use. There were some big rooms and some small rooms. She needed to figure out which after-school classes had the most students in them and which classes were smaller.

Can you think of a way to help Ms. Williams organize her data?

Ms. Williams looked at her data again and made this graph.

		Yama	
		Leo	Gregory
		Jacy	Rochelle
Malcolm		Jeffrey	Holly
Nate	Simon	Henry	Chen
Carolina	Leigh	Carla	Anita
Alberto	Esteban		
Art	**Music**	**Sports and Outdoor Play**	**Drama**

Which class will need the largest space?
How many more children are in Art than in Music?
How many children will be in the after-school classes altogether?

one hundred nine | **SMH** 109

A Line Plot

In school, you will collect data about how many pockets all the students in your class are wearing. You can represent the data on a line plot. Here is an example from one second-grade class.

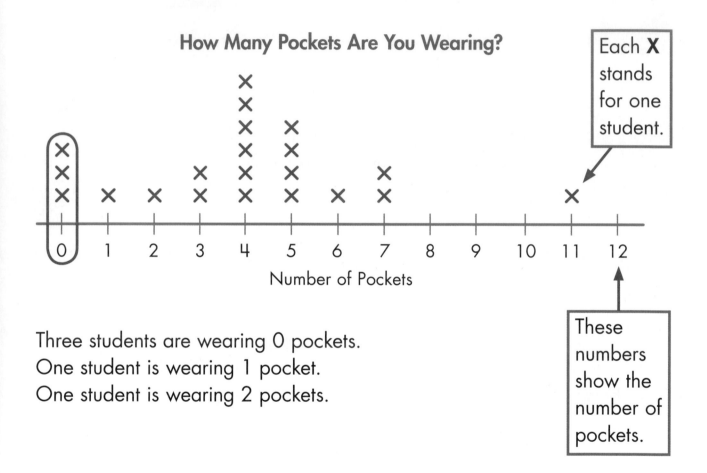

How Many Pockets Are You Wearing?

Each **X** stands for one student.

These numbers show the number of pockets.

Number of Pockets

Three students are wearing 0 pockets.
One student is wearing 1 pocket.
One student is wearing 2 pockets.

**How many students are wearing 4 pockets?
How many students are wearing 8 pockets?
How many students answered the question?
What else do you notice?**

Talking About Data

Here is the same graph about pockets.
Take another look.

How Many Pockets Are You Wearing?

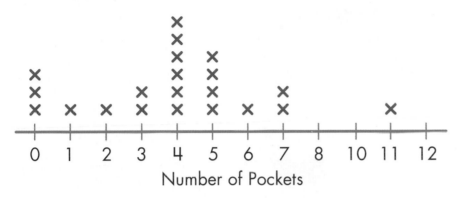

Number of Pockets

There are many words that you can use to talk about data
with numbers. Here are some of them.

Word	How It is Used in This Graph
highest value	11 pockets is the greatest number of pockets that a child in this class is wearing.
lowest value	0 pockets is the fewest number of pockets that a child in this class is wearing.
range	The number of pockets ranges from 0 to 11 in this class.
mode	The most common number of pockets is 4.
outlier	11 pockets is the outlier in this class. This is an unusual number of pockets.

Geometry

Geometry is the study of shapes.

There are shapes everywhere. We can find shapes in our classroom, at home, on the street, and in the world around us.

Look around. What shapes do you see?

Shapes in the World

 What shapes do you see in this picture?

2-D Shapes

Two-dimensional, or 2-D, shapes are flat. They can be drawn on a piece of paper or any other flat surface. Here are some 2-D shapes.

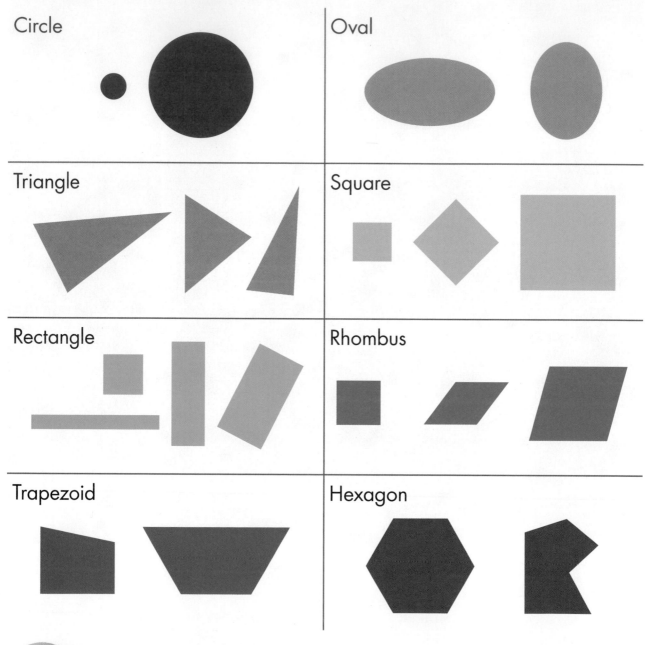

Circle

Oval

Triangle

Square

Rectangle

Rhombus

Trapezoid

Hexagon

Draw some 2-D shapes. What shapes did you draw?

Polygons

A polygon is a closed 2-D shape. All of the sides are straight.

These shapes are polygons.	These are not polygons.

Which of these are polygons?

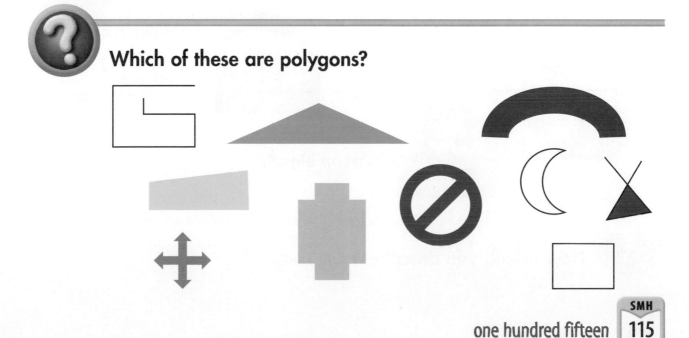

Describing Polygons

You can describe polygons by how they look. Here are some ways that second-grade students describe different polygons.

"It has 4 sides and 4 corners. The sides are slanted."

"It looks like a bowl. The top is wider than the bottom."

"It's a triangle but it's tilted, like it's falling over."

"It's got 3 points. The one on top is very pointy."

"It's like a circle but there are no curves."

"It looks like a stop sign."

How would you describe these shapes?

Naming Polygons

Polygons are named for the number of sides they have.

Triangles 3 sides	Quadrilaterals 4 sides
Pentagons 5 sides	Hexagons 6 sides
Heptagons 7 sides	Octagons 8 sides

**A polygon with 12 sides is called a dodecagon.
Can you draw a dodecagon?**

one hundred seventeen | SMH **117**

Sides, Vertices, and Angles

You can also describe a polygon by talking about sides, vertices, and angles. Think about a triangle.

A triangle has 3 sides.

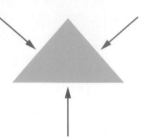

A vertex is the place where two lines meet. If there is more than one vertex, they are called vertices. (A lot of second graders call vertices corners.)

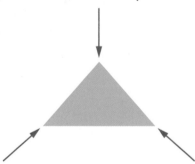

A triangle has 3 vertices.

When two lines meet, they make an angle. angle

A triangle has 3 angles.

 How many sides does a quadrilateral have? How many vertices? How many angles? What about a hexagon?

Right Angles

Math Words
• **right angle**

There are different kinds of angles. When an angle makes a square corner, it is called a right angle. You can fit a square into a right angle.

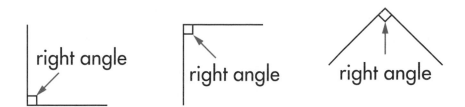

This triangle has one right angle and two angles that are not right angles.

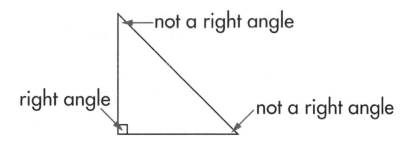

 Four of these shapes have a right angle. Can you find them?

Quadrilaterals

Math Words
• quadrilateral

A quadrilateral is a polygon that has 4 sides.

There are quadrilaterals in the world all around you. Do you see anything shaped like a quadrilateral near you right now?

These shapes are quadrilaterals.

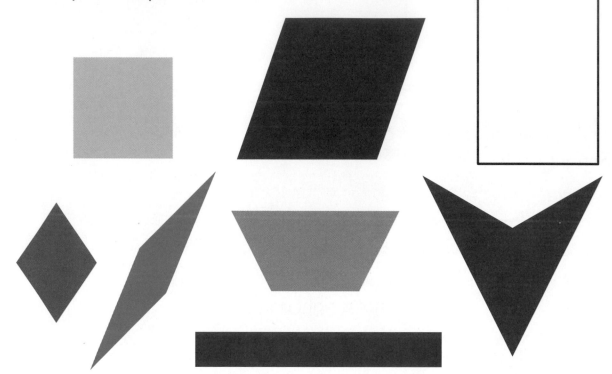

 Which of these shapes are quadrilaterals? Why do you think so?

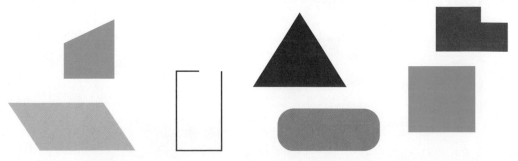

Rectangles and Squares

Math Words
• **rectangle**
• **square**

A rectangle is a special kind of quadrilateral.
Rectangles have 4 sides and 4 right angles.
Here are some rectangles.

A square is a special kind of rectangle. A square has
4 right angles and 4 equal sides. Here are some squares.

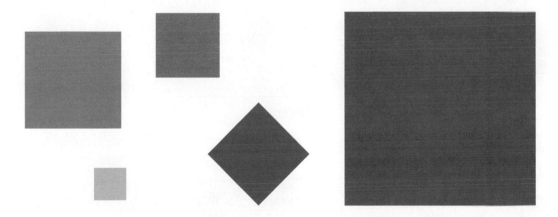

What is the same about squares and rectangles?
What is special about squares?
Can you draw some squares and rectangles?

3-D Shapes

Three-dimensional, or 3-D, shapes are solid objects. If they are small, you can pick them up and hold them. Here are some 3-D shapes.

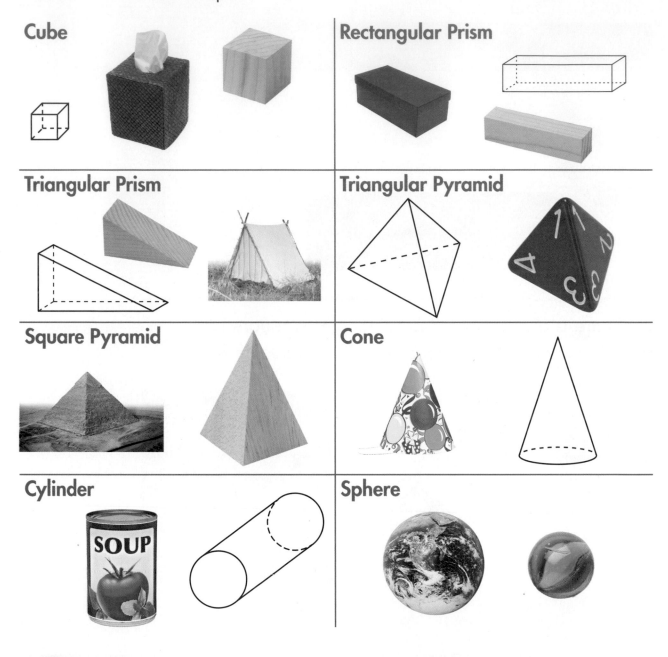

Cube

Rectangular Prism

Triangular Prism

Triangular Pyramid

Square Pyramid

Cone

Cylinder

Sphere

Look around you. What 3-D shapes do you see?

Drawing 3-D Shapes

It is hard to draw 3-D shapes on paper.

Here are some examples of how to draw 3-D shapes.

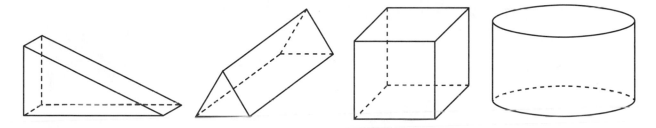

Here are some second-grade drawings of 3-D shapes.

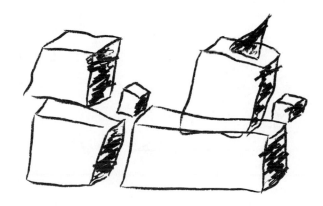

 How would you draw a 3-D shape?

Describing 3-D Shapes

(page 1 of 2)

You can describe a 3-D shape by how it looks.
Here are some ways to describe 3-D shapes.

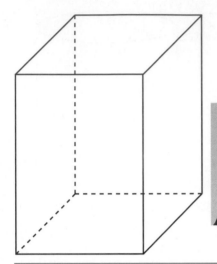

I see 2 sides that are rectangles and one that is a square.

This shape looks like a box.

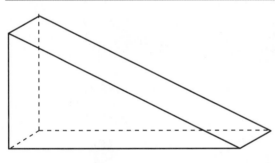

This shape looks like a ramp. It has 2 triangle sides. The ramp is a rectangle.

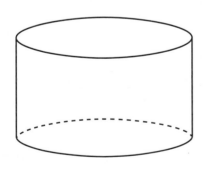

This shape is round like a can. It has a circle on the top and bottom. The sides are curved.

How would you describe these shapes?

Describing 3-D Shapes

(page 2 of 2)

3-D shapes have faces, edges, and vertices or corners.
Think about a cube.

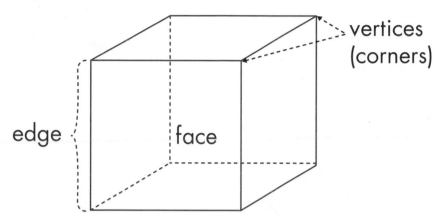

An edge is the line
or side where
2 faces meet.

A cube has
12 edges.

A face is a
2-D shape on the side
of a 3-D shape.
On a cube all of the
faces are square.

A cube has
6 faces.

A vertex is the point
or corner where
edges meet.

A cube has
8 vertices,
or corners.

**Look at this triangular prism. How many faces do you see?
What shape are the faces? How many edges? How many
vertices or corners?**

Rectangular Arrays

Rectangular arrays are arrangements of objects that are in equal rows and equal columns. Here are some arrays you may see in the world around you.

The same number of objects can form different arrays. Here are 16 oranges arranged in different ways.

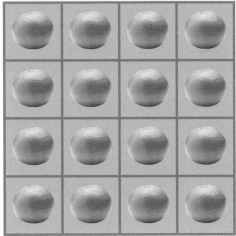

column

row

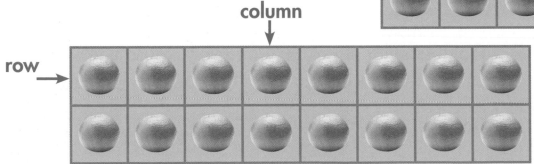

How many rows are in these arrays? How many columns? Can you find another way to arrange 16 oranges in an array?

Area of Rectangles

One way to measure and compare the size of different rectangles is to see how many square tiles it takes to cover them. The number of tiles used to cover a rectangle is called the area.

It takes 6 tiles to cover this rectangle. It has an area of 6 square tiles.

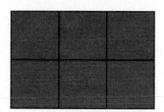

6 square tiles

Rectangles that look different can have the same area. For example, both of these rectangles have an area of 12 tiles.

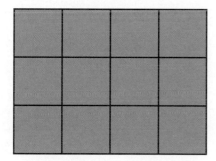

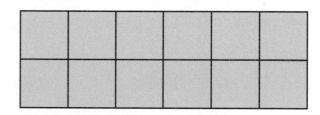

This rectangle has 3 rows and 4 columns.

This rectangle has 2 rows and 6 columns.

**What is the area of each rectangle?
Which has the biggest area? The smallest?**

 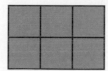 

Congruent Rectangles

Math Words
• congruent

Congruent rectangles have the same area and shape. It does not matter whether they are turned in different directions. Shapes are congruent if one can fit exactly on top of the other one.

These rectangles are congruent.

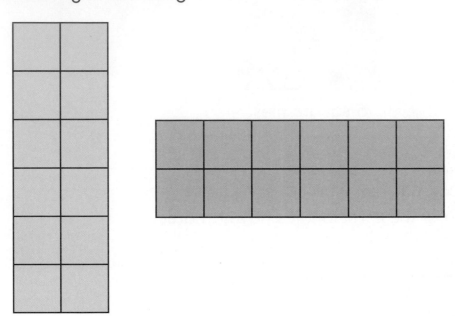

? **Which of these rectangles are congruent?**

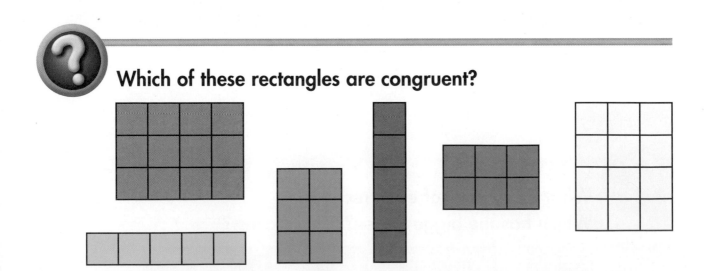

Symmetry

Mirror or reflective symmetry occurs when one half of a picture or object is a reflection of the other. A design has symmetry if you can imagine folding it in half along the mirror line and having each side match up exactly.

Some shapes or designs have 1 line of symmetry.

Some shapes or designs have 2 lines of symmetry.

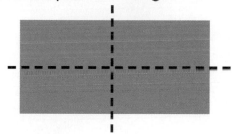

Some shapes or designs have many lines of symmetry.

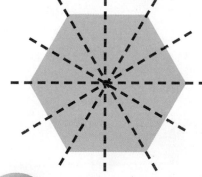 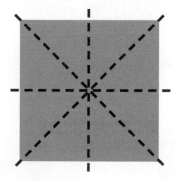

Can you find a line of symmetry in the shapes below? Can you find more than one?

one hundred twenty-nine   129

Measurement (page 1 of 2)

There are many types of measurement.
Here are some things you can measure.

Time: how long it takes to do something

I can tie my shoes in 1 minute.

Weight: how much something weighs

The baby weighs 7 pounds.

Length: how long something is

My dog is 44 centimeters long.

Capacity: how much something can hold

This thermos holds 2 cups of apple juice.

Measurement (page 2 of 2)

Perimeter: how long it is around something

The perimeter of my garden plot is 6 feet.

Area: how many square units it takes to cover a surface

The area of the floor is 12 square tiles.

Temperature: how hot or cold something is

Your temperature is 99.7°.

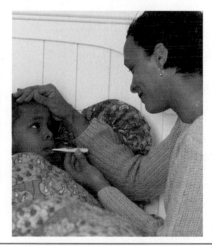

 What do you measure?

Measuring Time (page 1 of 2)

Time is measured in seconds, minutes, hours, and days.

How long is 1 second?		It takes about 1 second to say, "1 Mississippi."
How long is 1 minute?	There are 60 seconds in 1 minute. It takes about 1 minute to tie your shoe.	
How long is 1 hour?	There are 60 minutes in 1 hour. It takes about 1 hour to bake potatoes.	

Measuring Time (page 2 of 2)

How long is 1 day?	There are 24 hours in 1 day. When you wake up in the morning until you wake up the next morning is 1 day.	
How long is 1 week?	There are 7 days in 1 week. There are 5 school days and 2 weekend days in 1 week.	
How long is 1 year?	There are 365 days or 52 weeks in 1 year. From your 7th birthday to your 8th birthday is one year.	

 What takes you 1 second to do? 1 minute? 1 hour?

Tools for Measuring Time

Here are some tools for measuring and keeping track of time:

Analog Clock  An analog clock can have three hands to show the hour, minute, and second.	**Digital Clock**  A digital clock shows the time in hours and minutes.
Stop Watch  A stop watch can measure the time it takes to do something.	**Timer**  A timer can be set to ring after a certain amount of time goes by.

Calendars

Tuesday

September
12

Calendars organize time
into days, months, and years.

What clocks and calendars do you use?

Clocks

A clock is a tool for keeping track of time.
Here are two kinds of clocks.

Math Words
- **hour**
- **minute**
- **o'clock**

This is an analog clock.

It has two hands. One is bigger or longer than the other.

The big hand tells
how many minutes
have gone by.

The small hand tells
what hour it is.

This clock shows 2 o'clock (2:00).

This is a digital clock.

The number on
the left tells what
hour it is.

12:30

The number
on the right tells
how many minutes
have gone by.

This clock shows twelve thirty (12:30) or thirty minutes after 12.

What kinds of clocks do you have at home?

Minutes in an Hour

Math Words
• **minute hand**

On a clock, the big hand moves every minute.
It is also called the minute hand.

There are 60 minutes in one hour.

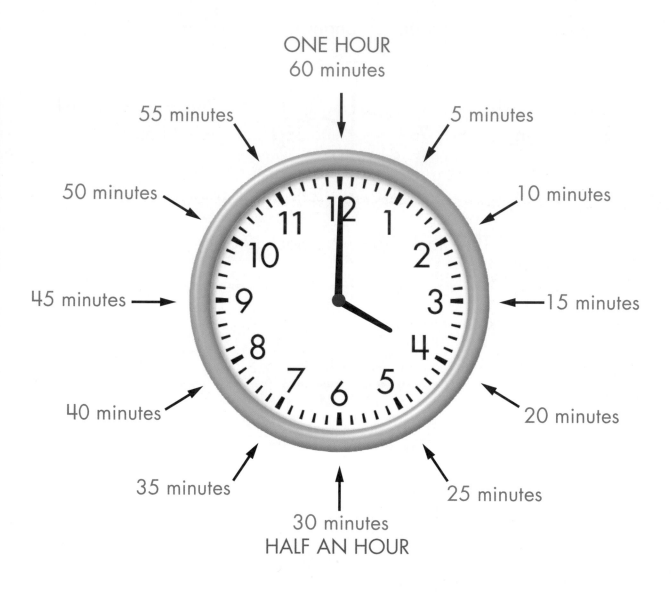

Parts of an Hour (page 1 of 2)

Math Words
- half-hour
- half an hour

There are 60 minutes in one hour.
From 2:00 to 3:00 is one hour or 60 minutes.

2:00 2 o'clock	. . . to . . .			3:00 3 o'clock

Where is the minute hand at 2:00?
Where is the minute hand an hour later, at 3:00?
Where is the hour hand at 2:00? Where is it at 3:00?

There are 30 minutes in one half hour.
There are 2 half hours in one hour.
From 2:00 to 2:30 is one half hour or 30 minutes.

2:00 2 o'clock	. . . to . . .	2:30 two thirty half past two

Where is the minute hand at 2:00? at 2:30?
Where is the hour hand at 2:00? at 2:30?

Parts of an Hour (page 2 of 2)

There are 15 minutes in one quarter hour.
There are 4 quarter hours in one hour.
From 2:00 to 2:15 is a quarter hour or 15 minutes.

2:00 2 o'clock	. . . to . . .	2:15 two-fifteen	
			People also say, "It's quarter after 2," and "It's quarter past 2."

From 2:15 to 2:30 is a quarter hour or 15 minutes.

2:15 two-fifteen	. . . to . . .	2:30 two-thirty	
			People also say, "It's half past 2."

From 2:30 to 2:45 is a quarter hour or 15 minutes.

2:30 two-thirty	. . . to . . .	2:45 two forty-five	
			People also say, "It's quarter of 3," "It's quarter to 3," and "It's quarter 'til 3."

Where is the minute hand at 2:15?
Where is it a quarter of an hour later, at 2:30?
Where is it in another 15 minutes?

Telling Time to the Half Hour

There are 60 minutes in an hour.
You can break 60 minutes into 2 sections of 30 minutes.
There are 30 minutes in one half hour.

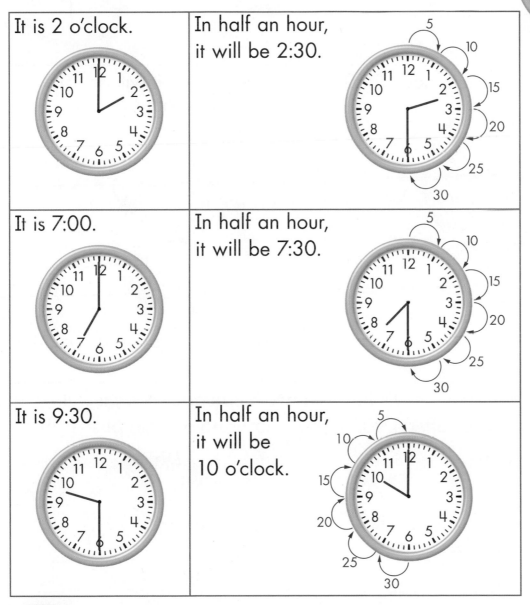

It is 2 o'clock.	In half an hour, it will be 2:30.
It is 7:00.	In half an hour, it will be 7:30.
It is 9:30.	In half an hour, it will be 10 o'clock.

It is 11:30.
What time will it
be in half an hour?

Telling Time to the Quarter Hour

There are 60 minutes in an hour.
You can break 60 minutes into 4 sections of 15 minutes.
15 minutes is one quarter hour.

This clock shows one o'clock (1:00). 	In a quarter hour, it will be 1:15 or 15 minutes past 1:00.  People also say, "It's quarter past 1," or "It's quarter after 1."
In another quarter hour, it will be 1:30 or thirty minutes after 1:00.  People also say, "It's half past 1."	In another quarter hour, it will be 1:45 or 45 minutes past 1:00.  People also say, "It's quarter to 2," or "It's quarter of 2," or "It's quarter 'til 2."

What Time Will It Be?

It is 2 o'clock.

In 15 minutes, it will be 2:15.

It is 7:00.

In 30 minutes, it will be 7:30.

It is 9:00.

In 45 minutes, it will be 9:45.

 It's 10:45.
What time will it
be in 15 minutes?

A.M. and P.M.

Math Words
• A.M.
• P.M.

There are 24 hours in one day. 12 hours are A.M. hours, and 12 hours are P.M. hours.

Times between midnight and noon are A.M. times.

Midnight 12:00 A.M.	7:00 A.M.	10:00 A.M.

Times between noon and midnight are P.M. times.

Noon 12:00 P.M.	7:00 P.M.	10:00 P.M.

 What are you usually doing at 8:00 A.M.? At 8:00 P.M.?

Timelines

Timelines are another way to represent time.
Different timelines can use different units of time.

This timeline shows hours and half hours.

School Day Timeline

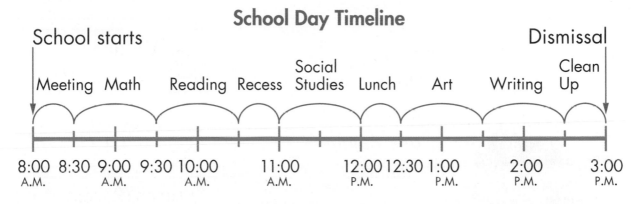

This timeline shows years.

Billy's Growth

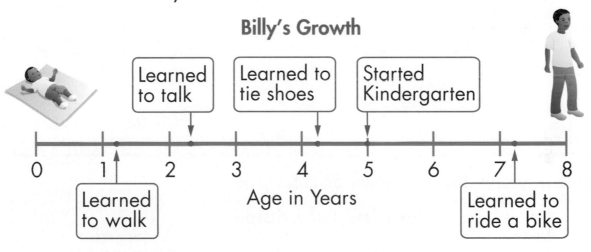

Here is another example of a timeline:

Life Cycle of Butterfly

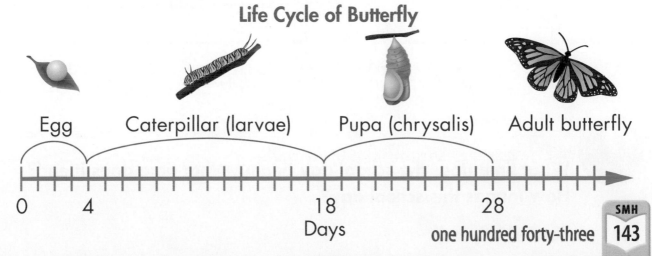

Representing Time

Schedules and timelines represent time.

Tuesday Schedule

Morning meeting 8:00 A.M. – 9:00 A.M.
Math 9:00 A.M. – 10:00 A.M.
Writing 10:00 A.M. – 11:00 A.M.
Reading 11:00 A.M. – 12:00 P.M.
Lunch/Recess 12:00 P.M. – 1:00 P.M.
Science 1:00 P.M. – 2:00 P.M.
Clean up 2:00 P.M. – 2:30 P.M.

Here is my schedule for one day in school.

This same day can also be shown on a timeline:

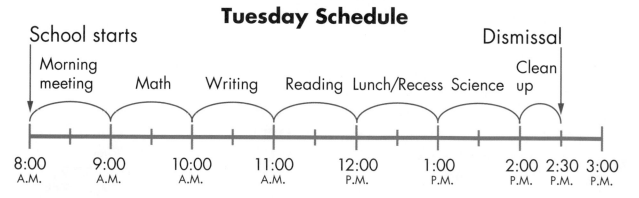

Tuesday Schedule

School starts — Morning meeting, Math, Writing, Reading, Lunch/Recess, Science, Clean up — Dismissal

8:00 A.M. 9:00 A.M. 10:00 A.M. 11:00 A.M. 12:00 P.M. 1:00 P.M. 2:00 P.M. 2:30 P.M. 3:00 P.M.

? **What time does the school day begin? What time does it end? How long is this school day?**

Duration

Duration is the amount of time that one event lasts from beginning to end. Looking at timelines and schedules can help us think about duration.

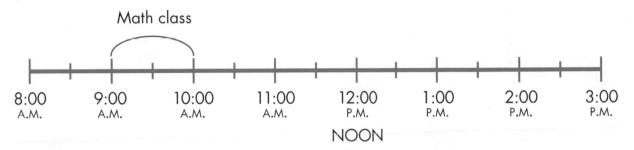

Math class

8:00 A.M.   9:00 A.M.   10:00 A.M.   11:00 A.M.   12:00 P.M.   1:00 P.M.   2:00 P.M.   3:00 P.M.

NOON

 If math class starts at 9:00 A.M. and ends at 10:00 A.M., how long is math class?

If you know the start time and the duration of an activity, you can figure out the end time.

After-school program

3:00 P.M.   4:00 P.M.   5:00 P.M.   6:00 P.M.   7:00 P.M.   8:00 P.M.   9:00 P.M.

 An after-school program starts at 3:00 and lasts $2\frac{1}{2}$ hours. When does the program end?

If you know duration and end time, you can figure out start time.

 Sally eats dinner for half an hour. She finishes dinner at 7:00 P.M. What time did she start dinner?

Measuring Length

When you measure length you measure the distance from one point to another. You can measure:

Math Words
- **length**
- **distance**
- **height**
- **width**

How far

This is how far I jumped.

Your height is 42 inches.

How tall

How long or how wide

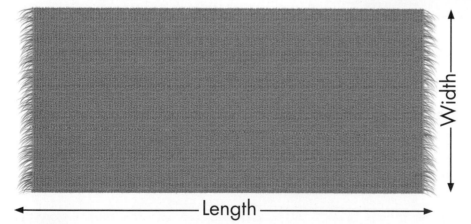

Width

Length

What lengths have you measured?

Measuring with Units

You can use cubes to measure length. For example:

Carla can line up several cubes along the edge of the book and count the total to find the length.

This book is 11 cubes long.

She can also use one cube and repeat it, counting as she goes.

This book is 11 cubes long.

Carla is using a cube as a unit. A unit is a fixed length.

If you are measuring with cubes, the unit is the length of one side of the cube.

length of 1 cube unit

To measure accurately, all of the units must be the same size.

You cannot measure a length with these pencils because the pencils are not the same size.

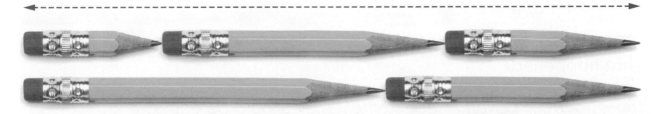

The count is different because the pencils are all different sizes.

Measuring Accurately

You can use units to measure the length of an object.

Length of 3 paper clips

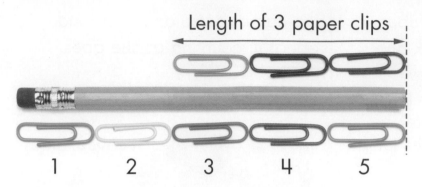

1   2   3   4   5

Travis used paper clips to measure this pencil. He said it was 5 paper clips long.

Nate said it was 11 paper clips long. What happened?

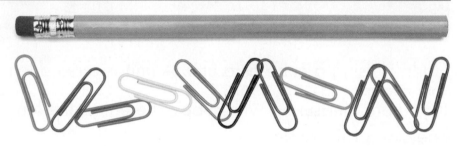

"The paper clips aren't lined up straight."

Rochelle said it was 4 paper clips long. What happened?

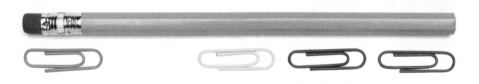

"She left gaps in between the paper clips."

Anita said it was 9 paper clips long. What happened?

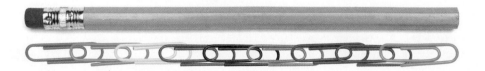

"The paper clips overlap each other. They should be end to end."

Half Units

This pencil is 16 cube units long.

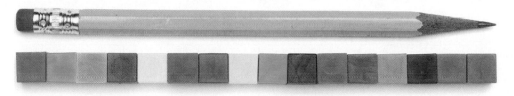

If a measurement ends in the middle of a unit, you count half a unit at the end.

This pencil is $6\frac{1}{2}$ cubes long.

This pencil is $9\frac{1}{2}$ cubes long.

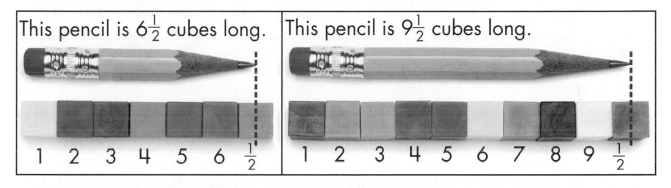

1 2 3 4 5 6 $\frac{1}{2}$

1 2 3 4 5 6 7 8 9 $\frac{1}{2}$

How long are these pencils?

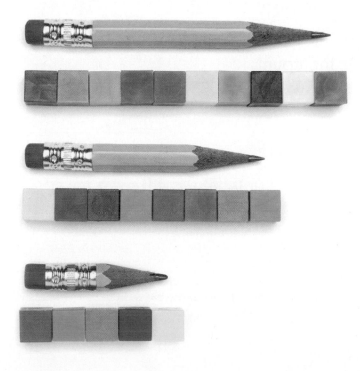

Measuring with Units of Different Lengths (page 1 of 2)

 a cube unit   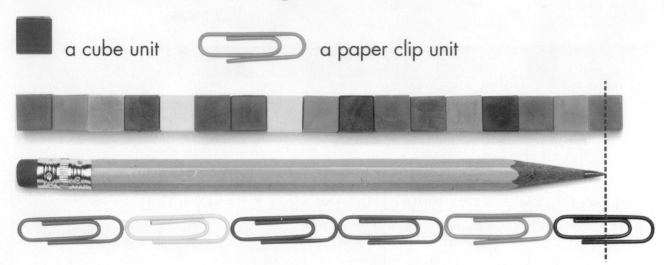 a paper clip unit

The pencil is $16\frac{1}{2}$ cubes long.
The pencil is $5\frac{1}{2}$ paper clips long.

When you measure, the total number of units varies with the size of the unit. A bigger unit repeats fewer times. A small unit repeats more times. In other words:

- The bigger the unit, the smaller the count
- The smaller the unit, the bigger the count

The same number of different-sized units gives different lengths. 4 cubes measure a shorter length than 4 paper clips.

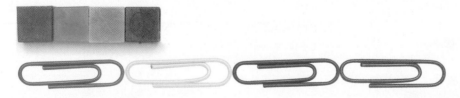

Can you explain why?

Measuring with Units of Different Lengths (page 2 of 2)

If you know the relationship between the units, you can use one measurement to figure out the other.

For example, 1 paper clip is the same length as 3 cubes.

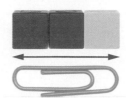

Then for anything you measure, there are three times as many cubes as paper clips. There is one third the number of paper clips as cubes.

This pencil is as long as 9 cubes or 3 paper clips.

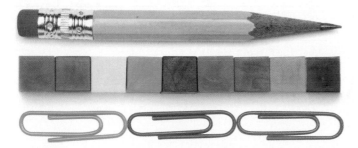

This pencil is as long as 15 cubes or 5 paper clips.

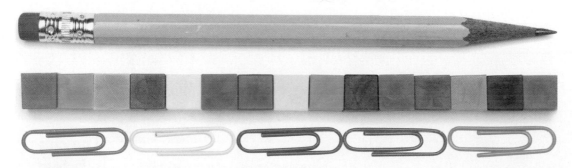

How many cubes are the same length as 6 paper clips?
How many paper clips are the same length as 20 cubes?

Using a Common Unit

When people need to agree on lengths and measurements, it is important that they use a common unit of measurement.

Imagine what would happen if everyone measured with units of different lengths:

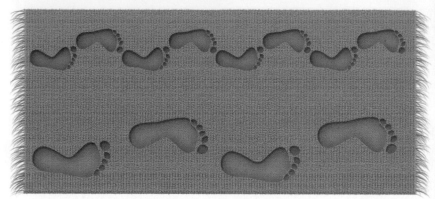

The rug is 8 feet long.

The rug is 4 feet long.

 Why did they get different measurements?

When people measure with common units they can communicate the exact same measurements and compare results.

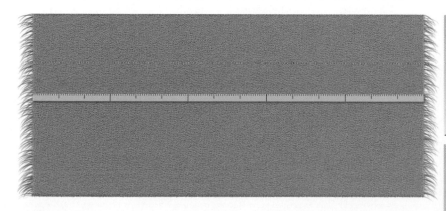

The rug is 5 feet long.

Standard Measurement

Math Words
- inch
- **foot**
- **yard**

People in the United States use inches, feet, and yards to measure most distances. Only two other countries in the whole world use inches, feet, and yards. Here are some things that are *about* the same length as those measurements.

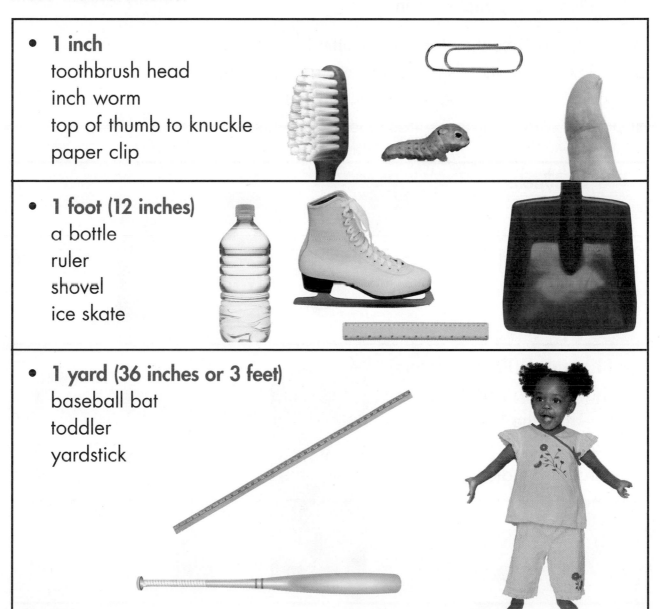

- **1 inch**
  toothbrush head
  inch worm
  top of thumb to knuckle
  paper clip

- **1 foot (12 inches)**
  a bottle
  ruler
  shovel
  ice skate

- **1 yard (36 inches or 3 feet)**
  baseball bat
  toddler
  yardstick

Can you find something that is about the length of an inch, foot, or yard?

Metric System

People from most other countries around the world have a different system for measuring. It is called the Metric System, and it uses centimeters and meters.

A centimeter is smaller than an inch. It takes about $2\frac{1}{2}$ centimeters to make an inch.

A meter is 100 centimeters. It is a little longer than a yard. A meter stick is useful for measuring longer objects or distances. Here are some things that are about the same length as those measurements.

- **1 centimeter**
  corn kernel
  lima bean
  top of pencil eraser
  ladybug

- **1 meter (100 centimeters)**
  height of a doorknob
    from the floor
  window
  broom handle
  meter stick

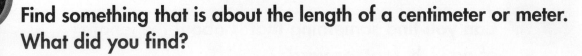

Find something that is about the length of a centimeter or meter. What did you find?

Measurement Tools: Rulers

A ruler is a tool to measure length.

This ruler measures inches.

This ruler measures centimeters.

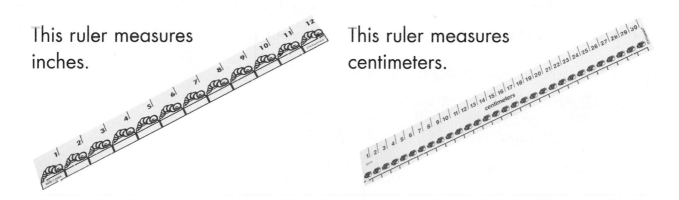

A ruler is 12 inches (or 1 foot) long. It is about $30\frac{1}{2}$ centimeters long.

This ruler shows inches and centimeters.

This is how you use a ruler.
This pencil starts at 0 and ends at 4. It is 4 inches long.

This pencil starts at 0 and ends between 5 and 6. It is $5\frac{1}{2}$ inches long.

Using Rulers

A ruler can be used to measure more than 12 inches or 1 foot. Start at the beginning and mark where the ruler ends. Then reposition the ruler so that it starts at your mark.

Holly uses a ruler to measure her jump.

Holly jumped 3 feet.

Darren uses a ruler to measure his jump.

I jumped $2\frac{1}{2}$ feet.

How far can you jump?

Other Measuring Tools

Here are some other measuring tools.

Tape Measure

You are 42 inches tall. That's also $3\frac{1}{2}$ feet!

Yardstick

It is four yards from the table to the door.

Meterstick

Almost all the doorknobs in school are 1 meter high.

Odometer

An odometer measures how many miles a car has traveled.

 What other measuring tools have you seen?

Games Chart

	Use in Unit	Page
Beat the Calculator	3	**G1**
Close to 20	3	**G2**
Collect 25¢	1	**G3**
Collect 50¢	3	**G4**
Collect $1.00	6	**G5**
Cover Up	3	**G6**
Get to 100	6	**G7**
Guess My Number on the 100 Chart	6	**G8**
Make 10	1	**G9**
Plus 1 or 2 BINGO	1	**G10**
Plus 9 or 10 BINGO	8	**G11**
Roll-a-Square	6	**G12**
Spend $1.00	6	**G13**
Tens Go Fish	1	**G14**
Unroll-a-Square	6	**G15**

Beat the Calculator

You need

- calculator

- deck of Beat the Calculator cards

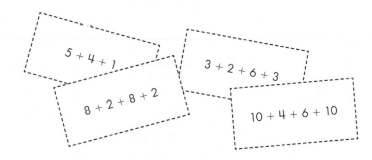

5 + 4 + 1

3 + 2 + 6 + 3

8 + 2 + 8 + 2

10 + 4 + 6 + 10

Play with a partner.

1 Turn over the top card in the deck.

2 Player 1 solves the problem on the calculator and records the answer.

Player 2 solves the problem mentally and records the answer.

3 Players compare answers.

4 Keep turning over the top card in the deck. Take turns using the calculator to solve the problem on the card.

Close to 20

You need

- deck of Primary Number cards (without Wild Cards)

- recording sheet per player

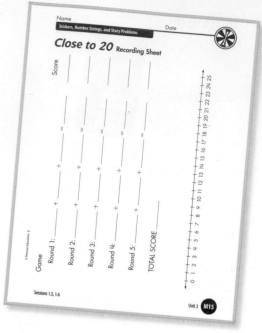

Play with a partner.

1. Deal 5 cards to each player.

2. Take turns. On each turn:
   - Choose 3 cards that make a total as close to 20 as possible.
   - Record the total of the 3 cards, and your score. Your score is the difference between your total and 20.
   - Take that many cubes.
   - Put those cards aside and take 3 new cards.

3. After each player has taken 5 turns, total your score.

4. Count your cubes. You should have the same number of cubes as your total score.

5. The player with the lowest total score is the winner.

More Ways to Play

- Play with the Wild Cards. A Wild Card can be any number.

Collect 25¢

You need

- dot cube or number cube

- coins

Play with a partner.

1 Player 1 rolls the cube and takes that amount in coins.

2 Player 2 rolls the cube and takes that amount in coins.

3 Keep taking turns. You can trade coins. At the end of each turn, figure out how much money you have.

4 The game is over when each player has collected at least 25¢.

More Ways to Play

- At the end of the game, try to make trades so that you have the fewest possible coins.
- Try to collect *exactly* 25¢.

Collect 50¢

You need

- two dot cubes   or number cubes

- coins

Play with a partner.

1 Player 1 rolls the cubes and takes that number of coins.

2 Player 2 rolls the cubes and takes that number of coins.

3 Keep taking turns. You can trade coins. At the end of each turn, figure out how much money you have.

4 The game is over when each player has collected at least 50¢.

More Ways to Play

- At the end of the game, try to make trades so that you have the fewest possible coins.
- At the end of each turn, try to make trades so that you have the fewest possible coins.
- Try to collect *exactly* 50¢.

Collect $1.00

You need

- two dot cubes or number cubes

- money

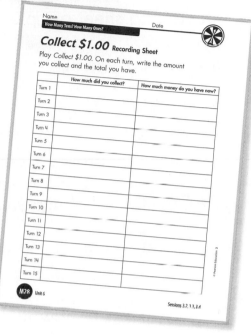

- recording sheet per player

Play with a partner.

1 Player 1 rolls the cubes, takes that amount in coins, and records the amount.

2 Player 2 rolls the cubes, takes that amount in coins, and records the amount.

3 Keep taking turns. You can trade coins. At the end of each turn, figure out how much money you have.

4 The game is over when each player has collected at least $1.00.

More Ways to Play

- At the end of each turn, try to make trades so that you have the fewest possible coins.
- Try to collect *exactly* $1.00.
- Play with a multiple-of-5 cube.
- Play *Collect $2.00*.

Cover Up

You need

- 45 counters
- recording sheet per player

Play with a partner.

1. Decide how many counters to play with. Both players write this number on the recording sheets.

2. Count out that many counters.

3. Player 1 hides some of the counters under a piece of paper.

4. Player 2 tells how many counters are hidden.

5. Player 1 removes the paper.

6. Both players count how many counters were hidden and record that number.

7. Keep playing with the same number of counters. Take turns being Player 1 and Player 2.

8. The game is over when the recording sheet is full.

More Ways to Play

- Play with stickers.
- During Step 3, Player 1 *adds* some counters instead of hiding some. Player 2 figures out how many counters Player 1 added.

Get to 100

You need

- two multiple-of-5 cubes

- 100 chart

- game pieces ⬭ ⬭

- recording sheet per player

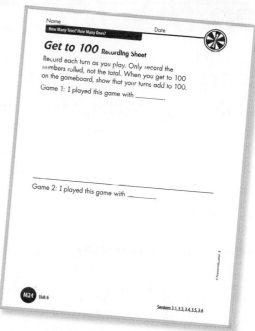

Play with a partner.

1 Player 1 rolls two multiple-of-5 cubes and adds the results.

2 Player 1 moves a game piece that many spaces on the 100 chart.

3 Player 1 records.

4 Player 2 takes a turn and follows Steps 1–3.

5 Keep taking turns. On each turn, follow Steps 1–3.

6 The game is over when both game pieces reach 100.

7 Add the numbers on your recording sheet to make sure that they equal 100.

More Ways to Play

- Play on a number line.
- Play *Get to 200.* Use two 100 charts.
- Play *Get to 0.* Both players start at 100 and move backward the number of spaces rolled.

SMH
G7

Guess My Number on the 100 Chart

You need

1	2	3	4	5	6	7	8	9	10
11	12	13	14	15	16	17	18	19	20
21	22	23	24	25	26	27	28	29	30
31	32	33	34	35	36	37	38	39	40
41	42	43	44	45	46	47	48	49	50
51	52	53	54	55	56	57	58	59	60
61	62	63	64	65	66	67	68	69	70
71	72	73	74	75	76	77	78	79	80
81	82	83	84	85	86	87	88	89	90
91	92	93	94	95	96	97	98	99	100

- 100 chart

Play with a partner.

1. Player 1 secretly records a number between 1 and 100.

2. Player 2 asks a yes or no question about the number.

3. Player 1 says yes or no. Player 2 keeps track on the 100 chart.

4. Player 2 keeps asking Player 1 yes or no questions about the number.

5. Keep track of the number of questions it takes to guess Player 1's number. Try to guess in as few questions as possible.

6. Take turns being Player 1 and Player 2.

More Ways to Play

- Play with a small group.
- Play on a number line. Use clothespins to narrow the range of possible numbers.

Make 10

You need

- deck of Primary Number Cards (without Wild Cards)

Play with a partner.

1 Deal 4 rows of 5 cards, with the numbers showing.

2 Player 1 finds 2 cards that make 10. Player 1 takes the cards and records the combination of 10.

3 Replace the missing cards with 2 cards from the deck.

4 Player 2 finds 2 cards that make 10. Player 2 takes the cards and records the combination of 10.

5 Replace the missing cards.

6 Keep taking turns finding two cards that make 10 and recording the combinations.

7 The game is over when there are no more cards or there are no more cards that make 10.

More Ways to Play

- Play with the Wild Cards. A Wild Card can be any number.
- Replace the missing cards *only* when there are no more pairs that make 10.
- Play *More Than Two To Make 10*. Use more than 2 cards to make 10.

Plus 1 or 2 BINGO

You need

- deck of Primary Number Cards (without Wild Cards)

- two kinds of counters (20 per player)

- gameboard

Play with a partner.

1 Player 1 turns over the top card in the deck.

2 Player 1 adds 1 or 2 to that number, and covers the sum on the gameboard.

3 Player 2 turns over the top card.

4 Player 2 adds 1 or 2 to that number, and covers the sum on the gameboard.

5 Keep taking turns. If all of the possible sums are covered, take another card.

6 The game is over when all of the numbers in one row are covered. The numbers can go across ⬜⬜⬜⬜⬜⬜, down ⬜, or corner to corner. ⬜

More Ways to Play

- Play with the Wild Cards. A Wild Card can be any number.
- Play to fill more than one row.
- Play as a team. Try to fill the entire gameboard.

Plus 9 or 10 BINGO

You need

- deck of Primary Number Cards (without Wild Cards)

- two kinds of counters (20 per player)

- gameboard

Play with a partner.

1 Player 1 turns over the top card in the deck.

2 Player 1 adds 9 or 10 to that number, and covers the sum on the gameboard.

3 Player 2 turns over the top card.

4 Player 2 adds 9 or 10 to that number, and covers the sum on the gameboard.

5 Keep taking turns. If all of the possible sums are covered, take another card.

6 The game is over when all of the numbers in one row are covered. The numbers can go across ⬜⬜⬜⬜⬜⬜, down ⬜, or corner to corner. ⬜

More Ways to Play

- Play with the Wild Cards. A Wild Card can be any number.
- Play to fill more than one row.
- Play as a team. Try to fill the entire gameboard.

Roll-a-Square

You need

- two dot cubes 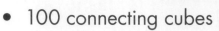 or number cubes

- 100 connecting cubes

- gameboard

Play with a partner. Work together.

1 Player 1 rolls and puts that many cubes snapped together on the gameboard. A row can only have 10 cubes. If cubes are left over, start a new row.

2 Player 1 looks under the last cube and follows the directions or answers the question on that square.

3 Player 1 says how many cubes there are in all.

4 Player 2 rolls and puts that many cubes on the gameboard. Remember, a row can only have 10 cubes. If cubes are leftover, start a new row.

5 Player 2 looks under the last cube and follows the directions or answers the question on that square.

6 Player 2 says how many cubes there are in all.

7 Keep taking turns. The game is over when the gameboard is full.

More Ways to Play

- Play on Gameboard 2.
- Design your own gameboard.

Spend $1.00

You need
- two dot cubes   or number cubes

- money

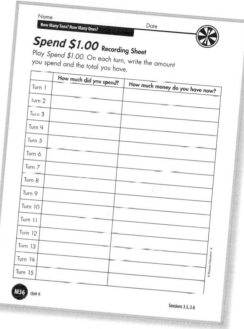

- recording sheet per player

Play with a partner.

1 Each player starts with $1.00.

2 Player 1 rolls the cubes and subtracts that amount from $1.00.

3 Player 1 records.

4 Player 2 rolls the cubes and subtracts that amount from $1.00.

5 Player 2 records.

6 Keep taking turns. You can trade coins. At the end of each turn, figure out how much money you have.

7 The game is over when players have no money left.

More Ways to Play
- At the end of each turn, try to make trades so that you have the fewest possible coins.
- Try to spend $1.00 *exactly.*
- Play with a multiple-of-5 cube.
- Play *Spend $2.00.*

Tens Go Fish

You need

- deck of Primary Number Cards (without Wild Cards)
- sheet of paper

Play with a partner.

1 Each player is dealt 5 cards from the Primary Number Card deck.

2 Each player looks for pairs from his or her cards that make 10. Players put down the pairs of cards that make 10, and they draw new cards to replace them from the Primary Number Card deck.

3 Players take turns asking each other for a card that will make 10 with a card in their own hands.

If a player gets the card, he or she puts the pair down and picks a new card from the deck. Their turn is over.

If a player does not get the card, the player must "Go fish" and pick a new card from the deck.

If the new card from the deck makes 10 with a card in the player's hand, he or she puts the pair of cards down and takes another card. Their turn is over.

If a player runs out of cards, the player picks two new cards.

4 The game is over when there are no more cards.

5 At the end of the game, players record their combinations of 10.

Unroll-a-Square

You need

- two dot cubes 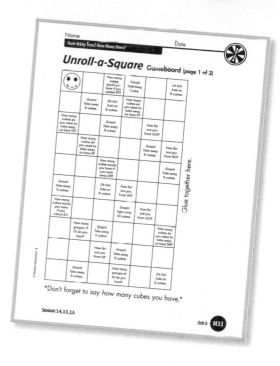 or

  number cubes

- 100 cubes

- gameboard

Play with a partner. Work together.

1. Place 10 cubes (snapped together) on each row of the gameboard.

2. Player 1 rolls and takes that many cubes off the gameboard.

3. Player 1 looks under the last cube and follows the directions or answers the question on that square.

4. Player 1 says how many cubes there are in all.

5. Player 2 rolls and takes that many cubes off the gameboard.

6. Player 2 looks under the last cube and follows the directions or answers the question on that square.

7. Player 2 says how many cubes there are in all.

8. Keep taking turns. The game is over when the gameboard is empty.

Illustrations

20, 101   Thomas Gagliano
30–91, 146–152   Jeff Grunewald
142   Jared Osterhold

Photographs

Every effort has been made to secure permission and provide appropriate credit for photographic material. The publisher deeply regrets any omission and pledges to correct errors called to its attention in subsequent editions.

Unless otherwise acknowledged, all photographs are the property of Scott Foresman, a division of Pearson Education.

Photo locators denoted as follows: Top (T), Center (C), Bottom (B), Left (L), Right (R), Background (Bkgd)

Cover ©Kris Northern/Phidelity; **34** ©Photos Select/Index Open; **35** Corbis; **84** (B, T) SuperStock; **86** (C) SuperStock, (B) ©photolibrary/Index Open; **87** ©photolibrary/Index Open; **92** SuperStock; **104** Chris Carroll/Corbis; **106** Steve Gorton/©DK Images; **113** Jose Fuste Raga/Corbis; **122** (BR) Getty Images, (C) Goodshoot/Jupiter Images, (CL, CR) ©AbleStock/Index Open, (BC) NASA; **126** (B) ©photolibrary/Index Open, (TR) Ian O'Leary/©DK Images; **130** (BL) Getty Images, (TL) Tom Stewart/Corbis, (BR) Goodshoot/Jupiter Images, (TR) Geri Engberg; **131** (TL) Getty Images, (TR) ©Royalty-Free/Corbis, (B) Ariel Skelly/Corbis; **132** (BR) Ken Sherman/Jupiter Images, (CR) Susanna Price/©DK Images; **133** (TL) ©Corbis, (TR) ©Royalty-Free/Corbis; **134** (TL, CL) Getty Images, (CR) Jules Frazier/Getty Images; **153** (T, TL) ©photolibrary/Index Open, (BR) Eric Glenn/Getty Images, (CR) ©Stockbyte, (C, B) Jupiter Images, (CL) Getty Images, (TC) Gay Bumgarner/Index Stock Imagery, (BC) Peter Gardner/©DK Images; **154** (TC, BC, CL) Getty Images, (CR) Corbis, (BR) Steve Gorton/©DK Images, (BL) Sagel & Kranefeld/zefa/Corbis; **155** Getty Images; **157** Leonard Lessin/Peter Arnold, Inc.